Prologue

This tale is part of the history of a tiny village called Cambridge, located some 40 miles northeast of Albany, NY. The village was incorporated in 1866, but the "crossroads" has been inhabited since prehistoric times. Paleo Indians used a system of trails down the narrow valley, while others, coming up out of the Hudson River Valley to the west, followed a narrow defile into the valley, and camped on the banks of the Owl's Kill brook to trade and rest before continuing east thru the gaps into the nearby Green Mountains.

Cambridge was once more economically viable than it is today. The days when milk trains twice daily carried dairy and other farm products directly to markets in Boston, Albany and New York City are long past. Having long been denuded of the old growth pine grove that, with rail service, made Cambridge a "destination" for city dwellers seeking momentary respite from heat and congestion, the Village remains the size (2,000 souls) it has been these past 100 years.

While no longer a tourist destination, it is inevitably converting to bedroom community, to which down-staters repair for weekend and summer solace.

Cambridge has always been a "one horse" town. Would it could stay that way. dt

COVER IMAGE: The ancient photograph displayed on the cover of this publication is of the Joe Sprague cabin at Sprague Springs, Black Hole Hollow. Altho there is a more modern cabin at that site, today only the step stone remains of the Sprague cabin.

Introduction

In October, 1898, the annual, County convention of the Women's Christian Temperance Union (WCTU) was held in Hubbard's Hall on Main St., Village of Cambridge, New York.

The Prohibition Party was then running candidates for public office. A meeting in the Hall in November was well attended. Coila (a tiny hamlet on the western edge of the Village) Presbyterian Pastor Rev. J.C. Scott introduced the candidate for Sec. of State, Henry Wilbur, who made a "plain speech for over an hour and possibly won the vote of a few 'doubting' Republicans". The Democrats, to hear Editor James Stevenson Smart tell it, were for no license requirements and wide-open saloons.

That election day, the Prohibition ticket polled 7 votes in the Town of Cambridge, 29 in the Town of White Creek and 15 in the Town of Jackson. The three towns occupied the southwest corner of Washington County in Upstate New York, and had formerly been joined as the "Old Cambridge District".

Who at that time could foresee the day when the Prohibition Party would shut down the booze halls of the Nation?

After a day of caucusing on the Prohibition question, weary citizens gathered at Scott's infamous "Raines hotel" (Cambridge East End) "for restful recreation after the setting sun had proclaimed...," etc.

By 9 p.m. the denizens were beginning to respond to the gentle ministrations of Scott's home-made lager and cheap whiskey. Tom Mooney received several gashes on the head from a spitoon, which attacked him without provocation, wrote the WCP satirist (likely Robert R. Law).

It also drove out the big window at the front.

The landlord himself had the meat stripped from one thumb by the teeth of an ungracious guest, who declined to be separated of his off eye.

Wrote Editor Smart: "Now who will have the heart to vote out of existence places so conducive to the refreshment of our weary and less opulent citizens?"

Under the Raines Law, Scott paid a $200 annual license fee to operate as a "hotel". That fee was totally returned to the Town government, which, as editor Smart feared, created an atmosphere of toleration for the intolerable.

Indeed, the present Town of Cambridge Hall was paid for with revenues generated by the saloons under the Raines Law.

The following week, Scott, the inn-keeper, wrote a letter in defense of his establishment.

Was this the only fight on caucus day, he asked?

"There were three rows, almost within a stones throw of each other."

His defense continued: "It is the fault of the rich citizens, who buy votes of the poor boys, thereby providing them the wherewithal".

With unerring logic, he concludes: "Knowing how the money will be used, who is responsible for the result?"

Perhaps it is not surprising that in that election, Town of White Creek stayed "wet".

Booze figures directly in the history of the Cambridge community. The rowdy nature of unrestricted alcohol beverage sales was one of the two major problems that led directly to the incorporation of the Village in 1866.

But as can be seen from these reports, drawn from the pages of the former Washington County Post weekly newspaper, which was edited and printed in the Village of Cambridge, the fight was long, raucous and not readily won.

And yet there were other, extra-legal ways to keep the forces of evil in check. Early Friday morning, the 22nd of April Scott's Raines Hotel went up in smoke and flames. It was a suspicious and very damaging fire, in that it burned off that section which is today known as The Hitchcock Block.

It was but a skirmish in the decades long battle to bring order to the chaos of the streets of early Cambridge. Scott would be back, as would his opponents, the ministers, legitimate businessmen, and fathers who sought a decent community in which to raise their children.

But foremost in the fight would be the mothers and daughters who, for most of the 19th century were forced to fight a "two-front" war; for as much as they hated the sale of alcohol for its debasing impact upon all they held sacred, they were also battling for an equal place in the world beside their fathers, husbands and sons. For while the Nation had fought a war with itself that cost a million American lives and resulted in ending slavery in the United States, the women of America remained without the vote.

In May, 1849, a Temperance lecture is carried on pages one and two of the WCP.

In December, 1849, Alonzo DuBois of Jackson gave a temperance sermon, that appeared on P. 1 of the WCP.

In January, 1851, when the Washington County Temperance Society met in Union Village, Sidney Wells of Cambridge was chairman.

A bill passed by the State Legislature in March, 1854 forbade the sale of any kind of intoxicating liquor by any except those licensed to do so.

The Governor vetoed the legislation, but the Towns of Washington County restricted licenses under the local option provision.

Irish had a rowdy St. Patrick's day in 1855. Crocker wrote: "We doubt (if St. Patrick looked down on us on the 17th) if he would have considered their riotous and disgraceful scenes complimentary to his revered memory.

"As is too frequently the case with the class of religious worshipper, after service, many of them repaired to the tavern, where they availed themselves of the privileges afforded them in the absence of the Main (blue) Law."   Drunk on rum, they picked a fight with the barkeep, and, grabbing a poker at the nearby fireplace, cleared out the joint. The trouble makers were arrested and fined $10.

Crocker wanted Prohibition.

The new local representative, James I. Lourie, supported that April, 1855 a new "prohibitory law", passed by the State Legislature.

The law set up licenses for the sale of alcohol for medicine, mechanical and chemical purposes and limited licenses for the sale of alcohol for human consumption. There could be one such license per school district.

The new law did not apply or restrict cider, except when sold in quantities smaller than 10 gallons and consumed on the premises.

Hannah Comstock, that May, reported that she had ceased to sell intoxicating beverages in her inn even before the new law.

All tavern keepers had to apply to the County Judge for booze licenses.

E. A. Loomis also stopped selling booze at his hotel.

In June, Albert M. Bininger of NYCity wrote a defense of the sale of booze. He made a living partly upon the importation of London gin. He opposed the Main Law.

By July, no booze was sold at Fenton's or Loomis' hotels. The Fentons installed an elaborate "soda" fountain in the bar room.

The new liquor law was hotly contested that summer. The "Prohibitory Law" was being strictly complied with. Editor Crocker reported no drunks on the streets in a month.

But there was already a powerful liquor lobby working against it. Crocker reported an Albany case where a violator had been released by a jury as "not guilty".

In the first local arrest under the new Maine Law, Officer C. McClellan brought in "a man named Robertson" before Justice H.K. Sharpe. Sharpe set the case for the coming Monday, but Robertson took "leg bail".

Estabrook's traveling railroad daguerian (photo) saloon was on the 8th of August smeared with tar and feathers, both inside and out. Crocker suspected that it was because of his stand for the Maine Law.

By May, 1856, the Prohibitory Law had been declared unconstitutional. Trafficking in liquor returned to the Village, including scenes of drunkenness returned after a years absence.

In April, 1857, a bill appeared before the Governor for his signature. It would license the sale of booze.

A New Excise Bill

The April 24 issue of the WCP carried the new excise bill on page one *in its entireity*. Commissioners for the county were to meet to grant licenses under the bill, which the Governor must have signed.

Page two carried an article explaining how to apply for a license.

The first commissioners for Excise in the county were appointed that May. They were Caleb B. Wells, Fort Edward; John S. Crocker from White Creek and Simeon Webster from Hebron.

Crocker drew the six year term, Wells the 4 and Webster the two. They granted a few licenses for grocery storehouses. Robert Rice of NWC got one. Located "opposite Loomis' Hotel", his was the only such license in Old Cambridge. The alcohol sold was to be for medicinal purposes only.

Tavern licenses went to E.A. Loomis (the old brick hotel), Hanna Comstock, corner Main and Park; D. Randall and H. Butts, all in White Creek. Zal and W.L. Fenton (the future Union House), E. Long (Checkered House), J. Green and H.D. Mosher, all in Cambridge. One of the latter must have been for the Center Cambridge Hotel.

No licenses were issued for Jackson.

The immediate result of the new liquor licenses was drunk-free streets. But by mid-summer, residents were once again complaining that their streets were regularly navigated by drunken men. The Editor shifted his aim from the Commission of Excise to the local constables, for not doing their job.

In August, Crocker called for the formation of a vigilance committee to close a filthy saloon operating in the East End. Crocker felt that incorporation would allow Villagers to police themselves.

Even Beer Licensed

The State Supreme Court that Fall determined that strong beer should be included under the new liquor law, and could not be sold without a license.

Editor Crocker found in the winter of 1857-58, "a marked improvement in the moral climate of the Village. This winter there was less public drunkenness and no visible 'dens'.

"The Sabbath was mostly respected. Even the hotels were patronized by the right people, not by the 'barroom loafer." R.K. Crocker was big on the "right kind of people" (meaning not "Irish").

For this, he credited the pastors of the churches and their series of lectures to the young men during the winter.

The illusion was shattered in late February, when a party of young men "from reputable families, so their names are withheld" ran riot.

Jacob Decker ("not always as temperate as we would wish," Crocker wrote,) entered the saloon on an errand. He came in contact with James Archer, "well-known rowdy of the Village". Archer pushed Decker out the door. Decker fell and while down, Archer ("this bulldog!") struck and kicked him in the face.

Archer was arrested and fined $10 by Justice H.K. Sharpe.

Weir's "so-called restaurant is a foul stain upon the character of the community," Crocker thundered. He appealed to the community "to take action against this hell hole!"

That March, J.B. Clark of Arlington bought the Fenton Hotel (Main and Union). The following month, Clark installed gas (carbide) lighting, as did B.P. Crocker in his storehouse. Clark would eventually have built The Cambridge Hotel.

In May, Crocker noted that local inn keepers paid $30 for their licenses last year, but "the little 7x9 hell holes all around them are dealing out the accursed 'rot gut' without so much as thanking the Excise Commission for the privilege.

The licensing was a farce, Crocker determined, "and now more want licenses than ever.

That July, Crocker changed his position on the liquor business, thanks probably largely in part to an ad, which Albert M. Bininger and Co. of NYC began running in Crocker's newspaper, the Washington County Post. It was for "Bininger's Old London Dock Gin".

"If only good booze had been sold from the beginning and no 'rot gut," Crocker rationalized, "There would be no need for laws and Temperance Societies today.

Besides that, the Biningers were an old and respected local family. "General" Bininger still summers at the family homestead,"
Crocker noted.

In August, a second liquor store opened in North White Creek, what the east end of Cambridge Village was known as before incorporation. Joel Loomis sold from his warehouse "20 rods north of the depot".

The Ranks Split

Crocker had become definitely not a prohibitionist. In May, 1859, he wrote: "We are not among that number who believe that a man who drinks his one glass a day is just as great a drunkard as he who drinks his ten. We hold no such radical idea."

What he 'held" was, that "pure liquors have their usefulness, while adulteration should be prevented.

"However, those who traffic should abide the law and not create low gambling holes in which to decoy boys and youth to a life of crime and wretchedness."

That June, J.B. Clark hosted at his hotel, D. Taylor, "the champion jig dancer of the world"; Andrew J. Leavitt, "unrivaled on the banjo"; and Syd Hurdis, "the Great Wizard of the South", all on a Wednesday evening. Evidently, on weekends they played to bigger audiences in the cities.

In Sept. 1859 there was a brutal bar fight on the Sabbath.
It was between two young men over a "fast" woman, the so-called "star-ship of the oyster saloons". The battle took place in the open street, not 15 rods from a church.

In November, the Star Saloon opened two doors east of the post office opposite Clark's Hotel. At that time the Post Office was on the West End. It advertised XX Star Ale,

Scotch Ale, London and Philadelphia Porter, champagne cider, soda water and Burdick's Beer, as well as segars (sic) and tobacco.

In December, 1859 Coila residents took preliminary steps to organize a Temperance Assoc. Rev. A.H. Newton chaired the meeting. A committee of five was appointed to draft rules and regulations and report at the next meeting. Rev. Henry Gordon had proposed the organization.

In January, 1862 the Washington County Temperance Society met at the ME Church, Ahira Eldridge presiding.

At 32 degrees below zero, on January, 3, 1860, the Coila Temperance Society was formed. John M. Stevenson, Rev. Henry Gordon and B.W. Walkley were the leaders.

Walkley, a businessman in North White Creek, suggested that the next meeting be held there. The Coila residents told him to form his own society.

In February, a Women's Christian Temperance Society met in the Old White Church, Park and Main.

Walkley apparently reactivated an "old" Sons of Temperance Charter. The group rented the hall over Walker and Robinson's "new store".

That same month, another ralley was held at the NWC School. Among the speakers were B.F. McNitt, Dr. Henry Gray and Abner Qua.

In April, another meeting was reported. Dr. Gray presided and Rev. Gordon spoke.

Later that month, the Loyal Temperance League met, Azor Culver presiding. Dr. Gordon was present.

In May, the County Excise Committee met to consider issuing booze licenses. Many had been issued the previous year. Editor Crocker noted that "a curse followed the liquor traffic". Petitioners against store licenses in Old Cambridge numbered 800. The

Commission passed a resolution rejecting all applications for store licenses. Seven applications had been filed.

In Greenwich, 1,200 signed petitions and no tavern or store licenses were issued there. The fight immediately heated up. Horses of Temperance men lost their tails and mains. Mr. Patterson, proprietor of the People's Journal, was (rotten) "egged".

That May, a "confectionary" shop opened in NWC, but used "sweet young things" lounging in the door as a sign. Crocker advised the new owner to sell candy and "make use of the painter's brush for a sign, rather than a thing (we will not say lady) encased in hoods for a sign.... We shall keep our eye on these 'colors'. a word to the wise".

John S. Crocker headed the County Excise Board. The Board received considerable pressure that June from "wets" wanting licenses. His cousin reported that "the Colonel and one associate stood fire until their opponents retreated".

In August, John Jenkins was chosen to lead the NWC Sons of Temperance.

The summer of 1859, David and Joseph Niles built a new hotel in White Creek Village. Holcomb and Dalton would operate it. It would be open in time to celebrate the Battle of Bennington on August 16. D.P. Sisson opened a new mercantile business there and a race course was also set up.

10/28 Peter Volentine purchased Comstock's Tavern from Widow Hannah and sold it Oct. 1859 to Mr. Houghton, son in law of Zal Fenton. This sets up Zal at S. Park and E. Main.

The District # 1 school opened that winter, having undergone renovation at the direction of Martin Hubbard. Both schools, the lower and upper rooms, were remodeled and refitted. The outhouses, fences and sheds were repaired.

In December, 1859, J.B. Clark raised a large public hall behind his hotel (soon to be called the Union House). The frame was up. It was to be larger than anything the Village had seen to date.

On December 27, the hall was dedicated. Both A.J. Whitcomb's and Burtt's bands performed. It was called the largest hall north of Troy, with a 45 ft. width, 18 ft. ceiling and an 80 ft. length.

At the end of 1859, Thomas Ellis purchased the Cambridge Valley house from James S. Robertson, to take possession April 1, 1860.

In February, 1860, the "old" Sons of Temperance revived in NWC. They rented the hall over Walker and Robinson's new store.

T his building was west of Clark's (Union House) Hotel. Robinson and Walker were partners in a tailoring business.

That same week, the County Temperance Society met at the white Presb. Church.

The Spring of 1860 featured regular Temperance meetings in the Village. Dr. Henry Gray would preside. Or Azor Culver. The "constant" was Dr. Henry Gordon of Coila Church, who always spoke.

That May, the County Excise Committee met to consider booze license. The previous year they gave out too many, Editor Crocker thought.

"A curse follows the liquor traffic," he werote. There were 800 names on petitions against store licenses in Old Cambridge. The Excise Board passed a resolution rejecting

all applications for store licenses. Seven such applications had been filed from NWC and Cambridge.

Greenwich had 1,200 petition signatures. No licenses were issued for stores or taverns.

There was a Templars of Honor, first organized in December, 1845. The Templars built a new temple in Greenwich, with 50 members. Its objectives were to fraternize without alcohol and help the needy in the community.

Nessy Champlain Monster

Nessy, the serpent-like monster of Lake Champlain, has existed as a myth for many years. This letter appeared in the Washington County Post in 1873:

Dear Sir,

When the thermometer pointed to 30 below, my mind took flight to a time when water flowed and mystery lurked just beneath the surface. It was printed in the Washington County Post in July, 1873, the editor having, according to the custom of the times, clipped it from the Whitehall Times.

In July, 1873 a party of fisherman on Lake Champlain near Dresden, observed a great commotion on the water. Something rose some four feet out of the lake. It resembled the head of an enormous turtle.

On shore, Gen. David Barrett reported a similar sighting. Barrett's son and a friend followed it while Barrett went for a gun. From the way it drew its body through the marsh, they thought it was an enormous serpent.

Several others supposedly reported sightings at about that same time and placer. Some thought it to be 30-40 ft. long. The sun glistened off silver scales.

Another observation came from a public highway, where passengers reported watching a giant serpent, perhaps 20 ft. long, slither into the lake and disappear. Its body was of greater circumference than the human thigh.

After the reports, armed parties out of Dresden took to the lake in search of the creature. It was speculated that its lair would be one of the inaccessible coves, such as Axehelm Bay.

The next week, the Whitehall New got into the act. The News credited the serpent with piloting Champlain, the first white man into the lake, and accompanying Ethan Allen on his historic excursion to Fort Ticonderoga.

The serpent became greatly annoyed with the British's attempt to maintain communications via the lake. It was with Commodore McDonough at the Battle of Plattsburg.

It was inclined to help the Union during the Civil War, but was so disgusted with the mismanagement of First Bull Run that the serpent turned "copperhead".

He sympathized with the Fenian raids on Canada following that war, but found the company too "scaly".

On land or sea, reported the Whitehall News, he moves at a stately 10 mph. He seemed partial to General Barrett's locale. Times were hard in the sea serpent business, too. Last winter he made admittance to the county poorhouse.

Intrepid hunters were to set a trap for the serpent, baited with calves, mud turtles and "railroad laborers".

In January, 1865, Editor Crocker went to work in the State Attorney General's office.

In Sept., 1865, as the Civil War wound down, the subject of Temperance heated up again. Rev. Isaac Parks challenged Editor Crocker's "moderate" views on booze, calling Crocker an "equivocator".

"I am anything, but," Crocker replied. He took a position against Temperance as a "political" issue, which, of course, it would become more and more as time passed.

This was a time of great unrest in the Country, but also a time of great religious fervor. Special trains brought thousands to a series of camp meetings held yearly at Eagle Bridge.

Dr. Parks, who was a Regent of the State Education Dept. at the time, took an entire column in the WCP to bash Crocker, who continued his defense of "pure, unadulterated, native wines" like those products of his advertisers Volentine and Bininger.

In November, 1865, John Hubbard had a fire arms sale at his warehouse. Evidently he had purchased a lot of surplus C/W arms. Among his best customers were members of the militant Finians, who were bent upon attacking Great Britain by invading Canada from the US.

A drunken row broke out on Thanksgiving Day, 1865 at Town's Saloon. A "bragadocious individual" received a severe beating at the hands of several young chaps who ought to know better than to be engaged in such disgraceful business," wrote James S. Smart, the new proprietor of the Old Washington County Post.

Officer McClellan happened by, but arrested noone. "The disturber of the pulic peace cannot be two (sic.) severely dealt with, and we trust that hereinafter, our officers... will exercise their functions fearlessly and promptly," wrote Smart.

Two weeks later, Officer McClellan still didn't have a "feel" for his job. "An Irishman" grew drunk in the saloon of E. McNitt. He was led outside by local rowdies, who then beat and robbed him.

In addition to being robbed of $7, a significant sum in those days, McClellan locked him up and fined him $15 for drunkenness.

Under the goad of Editor Smart, the officder improved. A couple of days later, Officer McClellan arrested one of the rowdies. It was E. McNitt himself.

Just after Christmas, 1865 a fire destroyed the storehouse of B. Pitney. The "fire dept." managed to save one barrel of flour and the front door. The building was owned by M.D. Hubbard, who was insured. This was Hubbard's first store-house on the site. He then built another where Pitney's had been.

The fire was an arson. The offender, lodged in the Bennington jail later on another offense, confessed when he thought he was dying. When he recovered, he recanted.

In January, 1866, the notorious character Charley Welch commenced a disturbance in the saloon of Francis Dickenson, near the White Presbyterian Church. Mr. D. stopped it and put Charlie out, whereupon, he struck Dickenson in the face; whereupon Dickenson gave Charley a sound beating and secured his arrest.

Editor Smart commended Dickenson, and bid all saloon-keepers to do like-wise.

Threshing must have been done in barns in those days. In February, 1866 John Maloy, employee of John Coulter of Jackson set a threshing record. George Cowan's record was 65 bushels of oats threshed in a day. Maloy bested that by threshing 70 bushels for Coulter.

"He is a sort of 'Sherman' among oat threshers," observed the former Civil War soldier, Editor James Smart.

Mason Prentiss was director of the Cambridge Cornet Band at this time.

That May, another notable brawl took place when three Irishmen assaulted a one-legged Veteran. One assailant was speedily demolished and retired, avering that his cousin who was killed last 4th of July didn't lose half as much blood.

The fight progressed, to the delight of a growing audience, until a citizen of the quiet Village of Coila, interfered and put a stop to it. The parties were arrested.

Patrick McGue was fined $10; Thomas Conolly admonished and bound over to keep the peace.

The Veteran gave bail for striking Thomas Cummings.

The row took place in the street outside the Union House, then run by Woodworth. Asked in court if they had gotten the liquor at Woodworth's Hotel, they replied in an outraged tone, "No. He wouldn't let us have any!"

The lack of control over drunks was brought home one Saturday evening in March, 1866 during a prayer meeting at the Methodist Church. A group of young men, all drunk, staggered in and took seats at the back. They began shouting "hallelujah" and "amen". The Sexton tried, but he was grabbed and shaken until subdued.

Finally, they drowsed off and were soon laying back dead drunk in the pews.

The prayer meeting adjourned and the Sexton remained to over-look the youths. Names were not printed because, sober, the boys apologized.

Fire Speeds Incorporation

Fire struck Cambridge Corners that March, and burned off the south side. It endangered the original Union House. Furnishings were carried out, but it survived. At the time, community leaders were deadlocked over incorporation. As this fire had to be fought with buckets, it tipped the scales in favor. While Temperance was not the deciding issue in the move to Village Incorporation, it was nonetheless a major issue.

A Vaudeville performance by trained dogs that April was disrupted by drunks. Wrote Smart, "The dogs contrasted favorably with some of the 'bipeds' in the audience.

"A man bred in the street and saloon, whose highest ambition is to be a loafer, and whose continual practice is to dwarf the intellect and debauch the body--- one would be ashamed to have the manners of a respectable dog spoiled by coming in contact with him."

Smart wanted an incorporated Village, with a good fire department and a strong "lock-up".

The next week, three boys were arrested for stealing from around the railroad depot. Two, Henry Donnelly and William McMurray, were sentenced to 30 days in the county jail as habituals.

"The wonder is," wrote Smart, "That more Village boys aren't ruined, the way parents allow them to hang out around the saloons and in the streets."

At the end of May, 1866, Editor Smart reviewed the Massachusetts slavery and women's rights movements. He had no sympathy for the "Black Republicans" who led it. "Truly," he wrote, "A band of pot valiant warriors. This is certainly an age of theorists and visionary dreamers.

"A strange anomaly, the most active period of our history, the most momentous crisis Republicanism has ever been called upon to pass brings to the surface theorists instead of reasoners, hot house rhetoricians for statesmen.

"The times demand a Cromwell; we have a Phillips and a Sumner.

"Times of agitation always throw the scum to the top!"

In June, 1866 E.P. Cramer began a cellar hole east of Hubbard's storehouse, to be

Cramer's store.

In June, Smart noted the resistance of German immigrants to excise laws prohibiting the sale of lager beer on Sunday. "How far can we legislate Sunday observances?" he asked, rhetorically.

"The Germans are probably as conscientious in thinking gathering at beer gardens to drink lager and listen to the bands as legitimate a way of observing the Sabbath as those of us cast in a sterner mould and dieted in our younger days on the shorter catechism, who learned to look upon the length of the sermon as the true test of its power."

"As a mere matter of ethics, the right of one man to drink lager on Sunday is entitled to as much respect as another's right to go to church."

The question is not a mere "jug-handled" one, he warned, noting that German immigrants "are the most orderly and the least inclined to intemperance and violence (when compared to the Irish)."

That June, B.P. Dalton purchased and renovated a large hotel at Eagle Bridge, to be operated for the convenience of rail passengers. A few days after opening, Dalton had occasion to reject further patronage of one George Sherman, who had gotten drunk and disputatious.

Sherman went home and loaded his wagon with stones. He returned and proceeded to "stone the fort", smashing the hotel windows and "things in general".

"Sherman persisted until the barkeep began firing back with beer bottles, which effectively drove Sherman away."

First arrested for public drunkenness under the laws of the recently incorporated village was Hiram Day, "an elderly gentleman, but prone to allow Langley's Bitters and Albany Ale to get the better of him."

Day stationed himself in the door of Henry Ackley's drug store on Cambridge Corners and "indulged his fluent tongue in an unwarrantable liberty with the names and characters of the customers," until Policeman Archer arrested him and "Hurried Mr. D. before the bar of corporate justice."

Being too drunk to stand trial, he was assigned to the new "lock-up" and the next day was fined $10, the first such fine under incorporation.

Charles Lewis and Wallace Decker, two drinking buddies, had a falling out on the way home after an evening of beer drinking. In front of the James McKie residence, Main and Academy. Lewis pulled a knife and stabbed Decker in the head. It wasn't serious, but Lewis was brought before Police Judge Gunn, who let them settle upon the payment of $50 to Decker.

Smart took exception. "This is all wrong. The crime is against society, and it is not the option of Decker to settle."

In another incident, which Smart said took place in The Cambridge Valley House (brick hotel, Park and Main), "one of the gangs who so frequently disgrace themselves and the Village they infest" turned upon and badly beat a young Irishman.

Their method was to first insult the man and try to provoke him to violence; then to fall upon him, knock him down and kick him into submission.

"Why doesn't the police constable make arrests?" Smart inquired. "If it is not too impertinent!"

Shortly thereafter, occurred the notorious "mayhem in Murray Hollow," in which one former Cambridge man (Sprague) split the skull of another (Weir) with an axe.

A "straggling band of fellows" were performing vaudeville at the Union House hall in July, 1866. Smart observed that "Their histrionic honors were not obtained by 'sock and buskin', but by means of burnt cork.

"It is not to be wondered at that the fellows blacked their faces. It was creditable to their modesty. But it was sufficient cause for the African race to institute proceedings."

"The country seems to be inundated with these bands, composed of men too lazy to earn an honest living. There should be a law to suppress them".

It took a while for the Village gendarmes to get the hang of it. Officer McClellan captured a man who stole $25 from George Wallace. On the way to court, they stopped at the Union House to warm their shins at the stove. The thief stepped to the bar for a drink, gradually worked his way around the corner and high-tailed it out the back door.

At that time, McClellan hadn't used even one of the six new pairs of hand-cuffs the Village had purchased.

Bored Wells

Hubbard and Maynard, at their lumber business by the railroad, displayed a novel well device that July. It was called the "bored" well, as opposed to the "dug" well. It was an innovation coming directly as a result of the technological revolution of the Civil War. It consisted of driving an iron pipe into the well and attaching to it a pump. Today, we know of it as "driving a point".

A number of homes still have in their basements wells driven with this new technique right after the Civil War.

In November, 1866 it was "publicly" disclosed that a whore house operated in Jackson. Late one night, shots were fired at some of the community's fine young men, to drive them from the Sam Scranton residence. One was hit in the leg; otherwise, it might never have been known.

Mrs. Scranton was fined $15 for firing the shots. She was also charged with accepting stolen goods.

Wrote Editor Smart: "If they devour one another this Village will be the gainer. It will not do to let the young men of this country grow up with no better idea of manliness than to participate in an assault upon a bawdy house!"

That same November saw the destruction by fire of Walkley's Store and the Union Hall, east of Fenton's Hotel.

L.W. Gunn, the first police judge under incorporation, was dying of inflammation of the bowels as his law office went up in flames.

In February, 1867 The Sons of Temperance secured a hall to themselves on the second floor of McKie's new building. At the same time, the Village expanded its police force from four to six constables, three in each district.

Woodworth's Hall (Union House) that March hosted Charles Pettengill's Minsrel Show and Brass Band. Shortly after, he sold the Union House to Ira Strout of N. Adams, Mass. Woodworth had managed the hotel well for the previous three years, Smart thought.

The Ides of March was marked by a free for all among Irishmen at the Academy corner. Heads were smashed. It got serious enough for pistol-shooting, which seemed to end the broil. Only a coat was perforated.

Patrick Brodie was the assaultee. The assaulters were James Bolan, Thomas McInerney and James MacDonald, who were charged with assault to kill.

By April, 1867, Editor Smart could conclude that incorporating the Village had led to relative calm.

Hotels Close

In June, 1867, Excise Boards operated under the rule that if a majority opposed licensing in a Town, no licenses would be issued. None were issued in Salem and

Greenwich. Consequently, the hotels closed, their livery yards were locked, and the owners threatened to make it permanent.

To counter this, Temperance Party members opened their homes and barns to travelers, and vowed to continue to do so as long as needed. One plan was to build a "dry" hotel.

Smart noted that Salem had to have a hotel, as it was a county seat and strangers had to go there; "but as to whether they are to have rum or not is purely up to the local citizens."

When tried in 1866 in Cambridge, he noted that liquor was sold anyway. So in 1867 the "dry" forces let it alone.

The Excise Board granted the following licenses in June, 1867: In Cambridge, Thomas Hill and Ira Stroud (Union House); White Creek, McDonald Cornell, J.C. Patterson, Julia Houghton, John Wright and Joel Loomis (store); Jackson, Lysander Wheelock, tavern; Salem (none; Greenwich, W.H. Waller (store).

In late June, the Ondawa House opened in Salem as a Temperance hotel to accommodate travelers. Smart predicted that the two hotels that had shut down to protest the loss of their liquor licenses would soon reopen.

That same week, a county-wide Sons of Temperance group organized at Salem, with members from Old Cambridge.

The County Excise Board in July reversed itself, and decided it could issue licenses even in the towns where a majority opposed them. Consequently, licenses went to James McNaughton and Howe and McNaughton and C.H. Allen (druggist) in Salem Village. Also issued were licenses to some hotels in Greenwich.

Smart was confused and outraged. "The interests of the public should not be trifled with!" he thundered.

In August, to commemorate the Battle of Walloomsac, E.D. Whitcomb directed the 7th annual ball. It was held at White Creek Village in the Hampden House, R.P. Dalton, Prop.

A.J. Whitcomb and A.J. Lake of the Peak Family Troupe, assisted by The Cambridge Band, presented a concert that October, 1867 at Union Hall. Wrote Smart, "It is useless to comment upon the ability of these artists, as their reputation is wide spread." There was a large and appreciative audience.

MD Hubbard and Maynard, that fall bought 35,500 bu. of potatoes for $10,000. They shipped 80 carloads, loading six a day. Two other local firms did nearly as well that winter, 32,000 bu. and 20,000 bu.

Local Minstrels

In January, 1868 the Village could boast of a minstrel troupe made up of negro juveniles. It was run by Donnelly and Legrys. Wm. Bockes was business manager. He arranged for them to perform at the Pumpkin Hook schoolhouse.

"The native Ethiopian talent thus recently developed promises to take rank among the first of the country," wrote the Editor. "We await their opening in this Village with no little interest."   Rev. Henry Gordon continued active in the Temperance cause. That month he addressed the Sons of Temperance in their lodge rooms over Wright's store. Later he lectured in the White Presbyterian Church on "The Pathology of Drunkenness".

The renewed interest in the old theme was in direct response to the undisciplined restiveness that descended upon the community following the Civil War.

In February, the Sons of Temperance of White Creek organized. Charles Starbuck was an officer, as was Pratt Jones, Sisson, three Allens, Turner, Bishop, Briggs and Butts.

Rowdyism still existed. In late February, three Irishmen spent the day drinking in Salem and returned in a belicose mood. They had in mind thrashing everyone, but instead amused themselves by throwing clubs at everyone. A warrant was issued for their arrest.

In March, the former WCP editor, RK Crocker, was appointed Village Police Justice in place of EE Noble, who resigned because of ill health.

In March, 1868, M.D. Hubbard was a key player in the building of a new 1st Presbyterian Church. The congregation was decidedly split on whether to renovate or build anew. Hubbard raised his pledge to $1,000 and the majority decided to push on for a new church, despite the lack of unanimity.

James Esman was allowed to sober up in the new lockup. He was in for disorderly, awaiting a trial when sober. He paid a $10 fine. By the WCP count, this was the third such use of the facility that winter.

By spring, 1868, Ira Stroud was in full charge of The Union House. J.C. Patterson was putting piazzas on the brick, Cambridge Valley House.

In March, 1868, N.E. Rice announced plans to build a new hotel on Broad St. just west of the depot. This would be the Central House.

In April at "Little White Creek", a "Daughters" of Temperance was formed. Dr. O.M. Bump installed the officers.

By July, the Sons of Temperance organizations boasted 125 members in Cambridge, 100 in Salem and 56 in White Creek. B.F. McNitt led the Cambridge contingent.

The Temperance movement even touched the lives of those local Indians who still lived the nomadic life. That July, a band pitched their tents on the depot grounds. But they "indulged in more fire water than local inhabitants thought proper; hence, their early departure".

That month, T.C. Gifford brought a complaint against Officer Rainey for being too zealous in his arrest of Thomas Smith for drunkenness. Smith, being drunk and abusive, when Officer Rainey told him to come along, he declined. Whereupon, Officer Rainey grabbed him by the collar and dragged him.

Editor Smart pronounced the judgement. "We give verdict that Rainey did right," Smart wrote. The complaint was withdrawn.

"Rainey is one of our most sensible officers," Smart finished, defensively.

Temperance by Race

No strangers to controversy, the White Creek Sons of Temperance were led off on a tangent of discord when "an African, a man of color" applied for membership. He was one James Dan, "professor of art tonsorial". In other words, a barber.

First he was voted in. Then came a vote to reconsider, and he was out. Whereupon, a number of members withdrew. The organization broke down and Dan was left waiting for the decision of a committee that didn't show up.

Wrote the late Union Artillerist, "Whether the committee decided it didn't need shaving, or that a gentleman of color should be wholly given over to the rum power; or whether they take the "Democratic" view, that the organization is a White Man's institution, we are not informed.

"The majority are in the right. If the young man wants in, he ought not to be denied. This prejudice against Africans is foolish and anti-Republican."

The next week, the White Creek Sons of Temperance admitted into full fellowship the African barber James Dan.

That Fall, as part of the campaign to elect Grant president, Henry Wilson, one of the Black Republicans of the Civil War, spoke in the park by the White Presbyterian Church. It was all a part of a great rally, including the Boys in Blue from throughout the county. Two bands and two drum corps were present.

At about the same time, Horace Greeley spoke at the county fair in Salem.

Judge of Discression

That Fall, "the War Editor", R.K. Crocker, fell at odds with the Village Board over the enforcement of the ordinance respecting order. The Trustees wanted drunks prosecuted to the letter of the law. Crocker had long taken a soft position on booze. As recently appointed Police Judge, he said that he had "discretionary powers." In other words, before his court, not all drunks were alike.

Crocker would be his own man in his own court, although only appointed to fill in. He would not be "a figurehead of the Board".

The Village Board argued that Crocker was not fining enough for drunkenness. Four brought before him were not fined the maximum.

Replied Crocker: "The four were guilty of having been born Irishmen, very poor, and with families dependent on their daily earnings for their bread.

"One," he continued, "Was guilty of being 70 years old.

"They, unlike the native-born, have no friends to hide their shame and so fell into the hands of the police".

He reiterated his determination to use his discretionary powers. Crocker reminded the Board that they had sought out him to fill the term after Justice Gunn died. He had not sought out them.

In mid-December, a "colored folks" dance was held in the Center Cambridge Hotel of T.W. Hill. A large crowd was reported, coming up from the cities on the railroad and traveling by omnibus sleigh from the Village hotels.

That Christmas, the reknowned black orator Frederick Douglas spoke at the white Presbyterian Church to a full house. He had a cold and a bronchial infection, which necessitated "a very quiet delivery" on the subject of "William the Silent," the great prince of Orange.

That January, a warrant was issued for the arrest of Robert Baker, who visited the Baptist Church of White Creek while drunk. He interrupted the sermon by "exhorting". Rev. George Brown was holding a series of meetings at the church.

In mid-month, Clark Mattison of "the notch" left one of the Village saloons in the company of Julius McCreery. When they had proceeded a suitable distance up the Ash Grove Road, McCreery clubbed Mattison to his knees, kicked him about head, chest and stomach, rifled Mattisons pockets and left him for dead.

John Curtis happened by and rescued Mattison, otherwise he would have died in the cold. McCreery was arrested and charged.

Death by Scholarship

At the same time, Hubbard Campbell of the Village was one of two Washington County scholars to win a scholarship to Cornell. The other was John Woodin of Fort Edward.

So desperate was Campbell for an education that it killed him. The tests were given at the county clerk's office in Argyle. A resident of Cambridge, Campbell took the coach to Greenwich. But the roads were bad and the weather terribly stormy, so that no coaches

were going to Argyle. He couldn't even hire a horse.

He set out on foot, reached Argyle, answered 23 of 26 questions correctly, won his scholarship and walked back to Greenwich. By the time Campbell reached Cambridge by return coach, he was sick from extreme exposure and exhaustion. Two days later he was dead. After friends thought him dead, he revived and exclaimed, "Hubbard is saved!" and expired. He was a recent convert to Methodism. He was buried at this father's in Brattleboro, Vt.

Christy's and Loraine's Minstrells, "a wandering band, exhibited themselves" at the Union Hotel on a Saturday night in early February, followed a week later by a ventriloquist.

The following week, in Union Hall, the Sons of Temperance performed the play "Ten Nights in a Bar Room". The editor thought the local cast well up on their parts. There were no unnecessary
delays to mar the show.

Russell's half of the then split Cambridge Band provided the music.

The residents of Salem proposed melting down a surplus bronze Civil War cannon to cast a life-sized soldier, the monument to be dedicated to the late Gen. Russell of that town.

They petitioned Pres. Grant, who replied that there were a lot of worthy generals, but not enough cannon to go around.

In February, a velocipede rink was opened in Union Hall, run by S. Sharp. It introduced the bicycle to the Village for the first time.

The times were decidedly unruly. In the post-war manufacturing center of "Pumpkin Hook", grateful citizens presented a new suit of clothes to one Benjamin Whitaker who single-handedly broke up a gang of thieves who had plagued the vicinity and annoyed the farmers.

That March, in the last lecture series of the season, reknowned humorist Petroleum B. Nasby appeared at the white Presbyterian Church.

In Johnsonville, Dennis Welch, a local laborer, was literally roasted alive in the saloon of J.H. Eccleshymer. The bartender accused Welch of having lice. He was forcibly stripped and someone poured "camphene" over his torso. Another denison set him ablaze.

A group of Vermont "toughs" took over Hitchcock's Hotel in White Creek. They threw tumblers to drive out the bartender, while Constable Butts hid.

L.L. Lloyd, a colored orator from Liberia, spoke at the Baptist Church that April.

Two neighbors, Asa Crandall and Andrew Wilson of North Cambridge, got into a dispute. Crandall knocked Wilson down with a club and beat him. Justice Wilcox of Easton fined Crandall $15, and he settled with Wilson for $50.

Strouds repainted the Union House and repaired the Piazza that May, about the same time Rice added another story and a French (Monsard) roof to his Central House.

M.P. Barton broke ground for his mammoth cabinet ware establishment (across from present bank).

That May, John LeBarnes got satisfaction from William Wells. LeBarnes was "ploughing" the garden of Russell Ackley in the East End one afternoon. He was slightly drunk and looking for a fight. Somehow the approach of Wells excited him. William declined the invitation to fight, whereupon LeBarnes split his scalp with a stake.

This did a fine job of attracting Wells' attention. He knocked LeBarnes flat. This seemed to satisfy, and LeBarnes went back to ploughing.

That June, N.E. Rice's Central House was denied a license to sell booze. Editor Smart wondered why, as it was no worse than the rest.

The "sauce" caused a highly improbable railroad accident that July. An express train Monday, July 6 on the Boston and Troy railroad collided with a wagon near Middle Falls. Aboard the wagon were Cornelius Tripp, a survivor of the Civil War, and Thomas Gibbon, employees of the firm of Adams, Bailey and Downs of Hoosick Falls.

Also aboard the wagon were kegs of black powder, freshly loaded from the powder mill. It was about ll p.m. when the express plowed broadside into the wagonload of gunpowder. It was one of the dug out crossings in that section, where the driver has little view of what's on the tracks until he crosses them.

The horse made it to the other side when the wagon was hit. Powder kegs flew in every direction. One swooped through the Engine house. Another, breaking on impact, covered the engine and ground with black powder.

The wagon was ground into small pieces. The powder failed to ignite. One keg was thrown 50 feet down the track and run over, and still it didn't explode.

Both men were thrown some distance from the point of ;impact. After a considerable search, Gibbon was finally found, unharmed. He had no memory of the incident.

Tripp was feared killed. The train brought him to Cambridge, where his parents lived, and he was carried to the Central House. He was treated for internal injuries and a broken hip.

Tripp was one of those with seemingly nine lives. As a boy, he survived being kicked by a horse. He was wounded five times in the Civil War. Now he had survived an incredible train accident.

Editor Smart thought it "altogether likely that both of them had been celebrating a little too much. Gibbon, it is certain, knew nothing after the accident and was quite stupid, and drove onto the track without thought."

Drs. Henry Gray of White Creek and William Stevenson of Coila attended Tripp.

Irish Improve

The Irish were steadily improving, in the eyes of the Native Americans. At the great grove south of the Village that July 4th, St. Patrick's Church parishioners held a huge picnic. The Cambridge Band played. Nothing stronger than lemonade was served.

Editorialized Smart, then a bachelor: "We doubt that any other nationality, American, Dutch or English, could show a better lot of fair-faced, pleasant-looking girls. Our Yankee girls must look to their laurels or their Irish sisters will carry off the palm for bright eyes and blooming cheeks.

"One could not help but think what wonders ten years had worked in the Irish population of the Valley."

By July, Ackley's third floor performance hall was about to open. Those supporting the construction of a church for the new St. Luke's Parish secured Russell's half of the Cambridge Band for a promenade concert there, even before the windows were installed.

The reviewer found it a bit too drafty.

Already, the rumors were circulating that a hall three stories up was unsafe.

In 1869, the Editor found that Shaftsbury, especially that portion bordering White Creek, had a class of inhabitants who, if not openly immoral, at least led lives different from "that Caesar wished for his wife---not above suspicion".

The Hill family ranked among the suspect. They lived in a house belonging to Samuel C. Wheeler in the edge of White Creek. Wheeler boarded with the family. Neighbors regarded him as Mrs. Hill's paramour.

For a considerable time, all went well. Then on Sunday, (July 4) Wheeler took sick. On Wednesday he died.

Neighbors wanted a post mortem, but Wheeler's mother would not allow it. He was buried.

Then a few days later, a child of Mrs. Hill sickened. Dr. Turner was called from Cambridge. He said the child had been taking laudunum (opium). Turner believed her poisoned.

The parents, the Hills, denied any knowledge of laudunum. Dr. Turner, however, found evidence, and carried it to White Creek Village. It had been put up for the Hills by the pharmacists Barker and Fassett but a short time before. It was supposed that some was given Wheeler and some the child.

White Creek officials wanted to exhume Wheeler and perform an autopsy, but he had been buried in Vermont, and they could not obtain permission from Vermont officials.

There was, therefore, some lingering doubt about the cause of Wheeler's death, but none in the case of the child.

The Hills maintained the poisoning was accidental, the result of sprinkling some rat poison on a pantry shelf and getting some of it on some pork, which was then cooked for breakfast. Everyone in the family had been somewhat sickened, but only Wheeler and the child had died from it.

But Smart stuck by his sources and his story.

About that same time, Brownell Niles, living near Center Shaftsbury, tried to murder his wife. He came home drunk and sought to force his wife to get drunk, too. She resisted, so Niles seized their child of three months and poured a quantity of spirits down its throat, strangling it terribly. Then he went at his wife with a butcher knife from the pantry. He sought to cut her throat. His first pass cut her on the hand and she rushed out doors.

team passed as Niles was chasing her with the knife. When he became aware of witnesses, he took to his heels and remained away several days. Then the family "reconciled". No legal action was taken.

About five miles from Bennington in the Town of Shaftsbury lived one Leroy Ellwell. He had been married a few years, although his wife refused to live with him. His marriage was not widely known.

Finally, smitten by the charms of a young, unmarried woman, Ellwell counterfeited a divorce decree and married her.

Lately Ellwell had become "possessed of the horror of his crimes" and imagined that the law was after him. Friday night last, he went to the garret of his own house and hanged himself.

It was the third suicide in Shaftsbury in seven months.

The "fusil" handed out in Hoosick Falls was also known to work strange deeds. One subject "of this delectable nectar" bit the nose off another, and "last Saturday night John Faley, stimulated by the same, got into a row with a saloon keeper of that Village and bit off his great toe.

"There is no accounting for the tastes of Hoosick Falls pugilists," reported the Post.

Central House Licensed

In late July, N.E. Rice celebrated his success in obtaining a liquor license for his Central House, "a triumph over his enemies, including the lumber merchant who, looketh after the vendors of liquors in this town." The quote from the Old Washington County Post could have referred to none other than the old temperance man himself, Martin Danforth Hubbard.

Working in Malachi Shaughnessy's blacksssmith shop that summer was Patrick O'Brien. Addicted to booze, he was often drunk and always abusive. One day he pushed Shaughnessy onto a pile of iron and pounded him a few times. Shaughnessy called Officer Chappell, but Chappell couldn't subdue O'Brien sufficient to hand-cuff him.

Volunteers were called for. James Finn stepped forward and O'Brien kicked him in the forehead for his pains. Clark Weir entered the struggle, ripping his best pair of pants.

Finally they cuffed O'Brien and got him into a carriage, but he kicked Chappell out. Weir and Chappell had to subdue him again. Judge Crocker sentenced O'Brien to a $15 fine and 30 days in jail.

Officer Baker was detailed to take O'Brien to the county jail in Salem. But Baker stopped at his home to eat first. He left a seemingly pacific O'Brien in the charge of his little girl on the front step.

"Good bye," he sez, and down the road he ran, Baker in pursuit. As he kept to the road, he was soon overhauled and landed in the county jail.

A great effort was made in these times on the part of booze as a medicine. That summer the local blackberry crop was reported outstanding, the fruits the color of blood. Editor Smart noted that some used it as medicine, claiming that blackberry brandy prevented diarrhea. "But the fact is," he revealed, "the only part of the blackberry plant that is an astringent is the root. There is no more medicinal value to blackberry brandy than in cherry bounce or any other of the tipples."

The Cambridge Lecture Assoc. had lined up for the winter perhaps the most prestigious program in local history: Windell Phillips, Mark Twain and Susan B. Anthony.

The lumber businesses of M.D. Hubbard and John Hubbard and X.Y. Maynard were to be consolidated April l, 1870. Hall and Randles purchased both yards. They were to take M.D.'s yard in mid-January, paying the market price for the lumber and renting the land. They were to pay $4,000 for John Hubbard and Maynard's yard and buildings, possession April 10. The Hubbard and Maynard building still stands at the RR crossing on Main St.

"Col. Randles, a Civil War officer from Argyle, had lived three years in the Village. J.F. Hall had recently moved to the Village. The C/W sword of "captain" Randles (ranks were commonly inflated after that war) was, in modern times, donated by his descendants to the Historical Society.

Rowdy 1870s

As could be anticipated, the decade of the 1870s dawned upon an unruly note. An assault was made on the chilled steel safe of the Cambridge Valley Bank that first week in January. But either the burglars were too inept or the safe too tough. While they failed in Cambridge, the next week they knocked off a Schoharie bank and then took the Glens Falls National for $20,000.

From December 29 through January 11, this band took upstate banks for $41,000.

Two murderers were being held in the county jail at Salem, although it had been 12 years since the last hanging. The new county courthouse and jail were ready for occupancy.

On Thursday, January 13, 1870, Mark Twain made his historic appearance at Ackley Hall.

On the 17th Petroleum V. Nasby held forth at the White Presbyterian Church, part of a rival lecture series.

On February ll, Susan B. Anthony lectured at Ackley's Hall.

The Cambridge Valley House was sold at auction to C.E. Stroud for $7,530. The Nation was in the grip of a serious depression.

In late March, the Temple of Honor dramatic troupe of Cambridge Village presented the temperance drama "The Drunkard's Warning" in Hoosick Falls. The following week they performed the melodrama in Ackley Hall.

In April, Rev. Blinn accepted the call to the 1st Presbyterian congregation.

In June, corner wars broke out over booze licenses. Two factions in the Village sought to control the liquor trade to their own advantage. An amendment to the Charter included an excise law to control the sale of booze.

The outgoing Village Board appointed an excise board, which licensed every saloon in town. The hotels rightly feared the saloons, with little overhead, would sell beer so cheaply the hotels would be left with little trade. The hotels cast their lot with the new Village Board, and did not apply to the old excise board for licenses. But two temperance men were appointed, James Ellis and J.R. McClellan, to go with Charles Porter, already seated.

The hotel keepers discovered that a circus was due to set up on the depot grounds at a time when they would be unable to sell booze and when no board could help them. "Deacon" Ellis wouldn't approve licenses for them, but he would resign in favor of a more understanding Solomon Fuller. McClellan would neither cooperate nor resign.

The upshot was that while the circus was in town the Hotel Union sold booze and McClellan and Porter, as a majority on the new excise board, awarded it a license retroactively.

Later that month, in William Miller's West End saloon, under Robinson's Tailor Shop, Police Officer Wallace Decker showed up at closing time and bid everyone stay, saying he had the authority to keep the saloon open. Miller desisted. The result was a general assault upon proprietor Miller, which continued drunkenly into the street.

Decker and Martin Welch were eventually arrested and fined for the incident. Miller sold out to Frank and Charles McMurray.

Editor Smart wrote that all of the saloons should be closed down, as "things have reached such a pass it is almost impossible to pass through the streets after I0 oclock without being in danger of insult and injury".

Things in the Irish Catholic community were quite different. St. Patrick's held its July 4th picnic in the big grove south of the Village, with no incidence of drunkenness. In fact, Father Matthew's Total Abstinance Society of Salem chartered a train and came down to join in.

The local Knights Templars, a temperance band, sponsored a series of revival-style meetings that July. Rev. J. Wesley Carhart DD was the speaker.

He called on the local churches to make it a crusade, with prohibition as their goal.

In August, the Town of Cambridge excise board declined to issue any booze licenses.

Cobbtown is Heard

Cobbtown was particularly rowdy in the 1870s. One day in late August, the estranged wife of Morris West was passing through, bound for Simpson's Spring. West leaped upon the carriage and proceeded to beat her about the head with a cobblestone.

Those who heard her cries and came to her aid advised West to flee into Vermont to avoid arrest. Dyer Baldwin, her father, started in pursuit. West was arrested and held on $500 bail for assault with intent to kill.

Editor Smart felt that special police should be assigned the inhabitants of Cobbtown and surrounds, especially on Sundays, in order to preserve the peace.

Murray Hollow was little better. That September, Lyman Gibbons and Luther Stanley met the 9 year old daughter of Morris Clifford as she was walking from her father's house to Shushan.

They "seized her, forced her into some bushes and violated her person, injuring her severely".

"What satisfaction can the law afford in a case like this?" Smart wondered. Gibbon was jailed, but Stanley escaped into Vermont.

Borrowed Wagon

Monday morning, Sept. 18, 1870, William Scanlon was drunk. Having "indulged too frequently at the flowing bowl, he was turned out of McMurray's saloon on the West End, and the major part of the day before him, he naturally turned his shuffling brogans toward the East End, with a plan of returning sometime to the tenant shack then occupied by his wife and children far out Annaquasicoke way.

It was roughly a mile, across spongy, sometimes muddy terrain, with narry a dram between. As he trudged the 100 yards past the old Wells storehouse, it grew decidedly warm. By the time he reached M.P. Barton's handsome new furniture warerooms, his toes were questioning the wisdom of his dull brain.

But the brain of William Scanlon was a work of Irish art. It rarely failed to find a remedy for the complaints relayed, however slowly, from the remote parts. A horse and wagon, the property of Monroe Conlee, was drawn up before Barton's.

It was by no means the the first time in the Old Cambridge District that a rig had been borrowed. Taking a furtive look about and seeing noone minding him, Scanlon released the reins, climbed aboard and kicked free the brake. He wheeled carefully across the rutty street and started at an imprudent gait for Blair's Brook and parts beyond.

He reached Dorr's Corners without mishap, but in turning the corner toward Cobbtown, the wagon over-turned. Scanlon sprawled across the inhospitable ground, bloodying his nose and scraping a large patch of rusty hide from his forehead.

Prudence dictated that he abandon horse and shivered rig and proceed afoot. However, the blow, coupled with the bowl, seemed to have addled his thoughts more than usual. The instinct of survival that so serves the dissipate failed him that day. He unhitched the horse, climbed aboard and started back toward the saloons of the East End, so precipitously passed by.

He met Officer Frazier on the dead run. Justice Crocker remanded him to Salem Jail in lieu of $1,000 Bail, although 50 cents would have done as well. Observed the fiesty Justice, Scanlon was "an old offender, who never passed a hotel without stopping for a drink". Or so it was reported in the Washington County Post.

The next month, a lively wedding party stimulated Editor Smart to another blast at the sodden little community. Stroud, the owner of the Irving House, as well as the parties who did the fighting, were released after posting $500 bail.

Smart: "Hardly a night passes, but drunken men may be seen reeling through the streets or reclining by the roadside. One was found on the steps of Barton's new store, asleep on the curb.

"But for this terrible demon, our police courts would have nothing to do. Bacchus could not wish for more followers in any one town than he has in this.

"The temperate man has rights which the intemperate is bound to respect... must be made to respect!"

The Lost Shawl

Clarissa Harrington lost her shawl. It was her only shawl, proudly knitted by some Old Cambridge woman of substance, who had given it to a negligent niece, who had left it unattended in the back of a buggy while she shopped in a Village store.

Clarissa had worn it that morning when she made a call upon William Scanlon, recently released from the custom of the county jail. She recalled clearly that she had placed it on the peg, just behind the door, where it would be handy and where, she thought, she could keep an eye upon it.

But when she was ready to leave, the shawl was missing. Naturally, she accused the people of the house. And naturally, they denied taking it, although none of the women of the Scanlon household possessed such rich trappings. And if they did, they wouldn't long, for such goods had a clear market value, and would soon appear about the broad shoulders of the wife of the local rum seller.

Clarissa nonetheless accused the people of the house. The dispute waxed hot and Cobbtown narrowly missed a "femalicide". Finally Clarissa withdrew. Leaving the Scanlons victorious in the word war, she transferred her complain to the Hall of Justice.

When the suit came up, Miss Harrington regained judgement to the value of the shawl. However, neither shawl nor its value was ever received, the Scanlon family having removed from Cobbtown to the Green Mountain State for the winter, the health of certain members having been given as the reason.

"We condone residents of Cobbtown for having removed the former resident William Scanlon." wrote the WCP correspondent.

"Evidently the rigors of the Vermont winter induced him to take the shawl with him. With the approach of genial spring, doubtless it will be restored," jibed the reporter.

Muskrat Theft

Tommy Livingston, one night in December, forced the chest belonging to an uncle and extracted 37 muskrat skins and a pair of rubber boots. Officer McClellan arrested Tommy, who was fined $10.

In January, 1871, the temperance movement formed "The Anti-Dram Shop Party".

Willard Nelson, that same week, drunk, "borrowed" a carriage to avoid walking home up the Hollow. But as he passed the residence of Mr. Qua, he steered into the fence. The carriage upset, pitching him on his face onto the ruts. Dr. Grey put his countenance back together.

Clark and Whitmore's Minstrels played to a large crowd at Ackley Hall. The reviewer thought them superior to most traveling at the time. End Man Hank White was "capital". He had new jokes and good acting. Clark, the clown, was "under a cold which hampered his vocal displays. The instrumental part, always augmented by A.J. Whitcomb's group, was fine, but the vocal work only so-so.

The Hurdler

The following week was enlivened by the tale of Tommy Smith, the livery hand. Having driven a party to Lansingburgh, he stopped in and acquired a bottle to accompany him back to the Village. It proved good company, indeed; for so distracted was Tommy that when he reached the railroad in the middle of the Village, he did not turn north toward Tingue's Livery by the depot, but south. He proceeded along Railroad Ave. toward a large steammill that was in 1871 about where Bentley's seed warehouse was in 2010. There was a 15 ft. drop in between, where 20 years before aggregate had been extracted for the laying of the railroad.

But Tommy thought he was turning into the Livery. He cursed and whipped the balky horse until it leaped to the bottom of the excavation. The buckboard was ruined, but the horse survived. It was a week before Tommy Smith regained consciousness.

That January, 1871, Editor Smart despaired, "That no man dare get drunk in Cambridge can no more be said; which could be two years ago". The "bloom" of incorporation was definitely off the "pumpkin".

"It is true, that we are no worse than neighbor villages. What is there to do? The responsibility rests with the people of the Village.

"Have licensees kept their trust? Have the laws been faithfully executed by the officers?

"What has caused this sad change?

"Intemperance threatens to sweep away our good name!"

Smarting under the criticism, Officer Robertson arrested J.C. Wright of the Village for selling rhubarb wine, in violation of the excise laws. The case was dismissed, of course, but not before poor Wright paid cost and took out a 6 month Federal license.

Henry Ackley, who built the hall on the West End and who ran a pharmacy on the first floor of it, was arrested at the same time for selling cigars out of a case, instead of out of the box. The "case" was dismissed.

"Both were trivial," Smart observed. "And the men who 'informed' engaged in very small business.

"This revenue business is odious enough to the people without any special vexations. We are not informed as to the complainant, but if he be a reader of the Post, we tender him the advise (sic.) to turn to making a respectable livelihood by the labor of his hands."

George M. McKie of Jackson purchased the interest of Warren Norton in the firm of Norton and Nicholson (tinsmith and hardware, where Hitchcock Block would be). Mrs. George had built the Danny Foster house.

He planned, with Joel Loomis, to build a brick block in place of the then ugly, wooden one.

Cady Stanton

Elizabeth Cady Stanton, speaking at the 1st Presbyterian Church in the Masons' winter lecture series, in Cambridge Village February, 1871, said, "The word 'male' should be stricken from the constitution of this state.

"Republicans had said that when they were through with 'Sambo' they would attend to the women. I would have thought that women were good enough to GO WITH 'Sambo".

In mid-February, a committee met at B.P. Crocker's storehouse to consider building a hall centrally located in the Village. Present were J.N. Hodge, recent unsuccessful candidate for Village president; James Ellis and J.N. Smith.

That spring election saw anti-booze candidates succeed. The hotel lobby in Town of Cambridge failed to unseat Dimick, the supervisor. The town excise committee had issued no licenses the previous year and would hold true following the election. The Town left it up to the Village to regulate the Union House.

In the meantime, the Center Cambridge Hotel was sold by Thomas Hill to Kenyon

Ingraham for $1,500. Its days were numbered.

At the hotel operation, L.F. Willet "held the last dance ever to be held in Center Cambridge." He would shortly close, "sine die' on account of the anti-liquor proclivities of the Cambridge Excise Board."

Thomas Sheehey, Irishman, was arrested on complaint of Proprietor Stroud of the Irving House. It took a large contingent to put him in the lock-up. His friends paid a $10 fine and costs.

Observed the Editor, "Thomas thought he would be too much for the corporation. He is a wiser man".

Whitcomb Music Man

By April, 1871, A.J. Whitcomb was managing the Peak Family Bell Ringers. In May they sold out Ackley Hall. The Reviewer noted that under Whitcomb's leadership, bell ringing took a back seat to the concert. A.J. announced that he was ceasing to travel with the Peake Family and instead would unite with brother E.D. and play for local dances.

The new Village regime resulted in the closing (temporarily) of all hotel bars and saloons. They expected to be back in action in a month.

In October, 1871, Madame Rentz brought her "Creole Troupe" of female minstrels to Ackley Hall. It was not a show of "legs", the advertisement explained, and was guaranteed not to offend the most chaste.

In November, John and James Garrity got drunk on "All Saints Day" and in the middle of Broad St. opposite the depot, kicked in the face of one Thomas Christopher.

When they appeared before Judge Leonard Fletcher, they refused to pay $10 fines. Fletcher sent them to Salem jail.

Mayhem in the Village

The 1870s continued to be a period of semi-lawlessness in the Old Cambridge District. This was, in part, because of the serious down-turn in the National economy. Other causes were the late war, the ineffective laws that were supposed to control the liquor trade, and the great number of recent immigrants among us.

Edward Callery, in mid-January, 1872, proclaimed that he was the victim of highway robbery. Said crime was to have occurred along the railroad south of B.P. Crocker's Storehouse. The said perpetrators were three from well-known local families, John Birmingham, William Wells and James McClellan.

When the case went to court, Leonard Fletcher, assisted by the venerable H.K. Sharpe, prosecuted for the State. The current dominant legal star, D. M. Westfall represented the accused.

Houghton was managing the Union House at that time. After sharing a drink, Birmingham and Callery, left together at 9 p.m.

They proceeded down Main St. and up Broad to the Central House, where Callery again treated. He opened his pocket book sufficient to show that he was carrying a large roll of bills.

The story of the prosecution was that Birmingham left the bar and called out Wells and McClellan for a confab. Afterwards, the parties returned to the barroom.

Birmingham told Callery that he had called a police officer and would escort Callery safely home, lest he be robbed of his money on the dark and muddy thoroughfares of the community.

When the pair left the bar, Wells and McClellan followed in their rear. When they had walked south past the Crocker building, Birmingham dropped back to talk to the "escorts".

Callery turned to see what was going on and was knocked down and jumped upon by one man, while another rifled his pockets.

While the person who had leaped upon him pounded his head against the ground to stop him, Callery yelled, "murder".

Having gotten the money, the men fled. The three returned to The Central House, while Callery wandered up and down Main St. hallowing murder. But who would listen to so drunken and disheveled an Irishman?

Callery could not identify Wells or McClellan. No defense was offered before Judge Crocker, who bound the case over to the Grand Jury.

Editor Smart noted that circumstantial evidence tended to point to the guilt of the accused, but "the public should remember that they are entitled to the benefit of the doubt until the final trial."

And on a fitting temperance note, "The predicament of Young Wells and McClellan is a warning to all of the dangers of intoxication".

The three were charged with highway robbery and assault with intent to kill, and were freed on $500 bond each.

Lectured the Editor of the Old WCP, In the past weeks three village families have been brought anquish by young men committing a crime induced by rum. One (Birmingham) was in the Troy jail and two were in Salem.

In March, Birmingham, James McClellan and William Wells were convicted and sentenced to five years at hard labor at Clinton Prison. It was particularly hard on the senior McClellan, who was a leading temperance man of the community. He would never recover from the disgrace.

In April, McClellan and Wells were taken to Clinton Prison to begin serving their time.

By June, locals were circulating a petition asking the Gov. to pardon Wells.

A year later, old Edward Callery died of the injuries which he sustained in the assault.

A year after that, in January, 1874, James McClellan Jr. was pardoned by the Governor of New York.

Father Fedigan of St. Patrick's continued to work on the image of the Irish. At a "Grand Union Fair" that January, he raised $3,000 for the Church. The good Augustinian noted that it showed that Irishman could meet and have fun without getting drunk and fighting.

Responded the Old WCP, recently elected to the U.S. House of Representatives: "If Father Fedigan had been disposed to play the Jew, he might have reaped a much handsomer sum."

That month, Charles E. Stroud sold the Irving House to T. Sanford of Castleton, NY for $23,000.

The woodwork on the new, 1st Presbyterian Church was complete. A bell from the Jones Foundry of Troy arrived on January 8. It was hoisted to the steeple. It weighed 2,500 lb.

A month later, Editor Smart suggested that it be sent back. It could hardly be heard at the Post building, a quarter mile distant. The congregation agreed. They rejected the bell and bought a more expensive one.

The Post editor, noting the increase in murder and mayhem, suggested that "A little hanging is the most wholesome remedy".

Zal Fenton offered this "hog story":

He had six pigs in May of 1871. Fatted on one acre of corn, they dressed out at 1,100 lb. combined weight, and "Uncle Zal" still had 15 bushels of corn left.

Patrick Welch, chopping wood that winter on the Henry Coulter farm in McKie Hollow, had a tree fall on him and kill him.

Fatal Sleigh Ride

Coming home from a Singing School in Greenwich, quite a few local young people were traveling behind two teams. One was smooth shod. The road was icy and coming down a hill the driver wanted the others to let him pass so that he could keep his horses moving smoothly. But the wagon of kids ahead were singing so loudly he wasn't heard. He had to pull up his horses and they slipped. They fell and rolled over an embankment, taking carriage and riders with them.

John, 15 year old son of Morrison Arnott, fell against a stump fence and his skull was perforated. He died in 24 hr.

There was considerable theft of robes and whips from buggies during a union service at Coila Church at the end of January.

One new law required that druggists affix labels to the containers of medicines, etc. which they sold. Henry Ackley didn't and a woman almost died. Ackley sold a bottle of Oil of Tansy to a woman and didn't label it poison. The woman swallowed a dram trying to induce an abortion. A physician induced vomiting and saved her life.

In February, the Post noted that the depot was besieged by more "runners" than passengers. The "runner's" job was to try to talk visitors into using one of the several hotels then available.

Orrin Kellogg died that February, at the daughter of his daughter, Mrs. James Buel in NY City.

Kellogg was born in 1786 at Williamstown, Mass. He came to the Village as a young man. A carpenter, he built the former Gilmore House of Coila, which had burned.

He married a school teacher in Jackson, farmed in Williamstown for 12 years, then returned to the Village and went into the mercantile business with Dan Rice. He was a constant resident thereafter.

He was an original director of the Cambridge Valley Bank and president of the board, a post which he held until age stopped him in 1870. Martin I. Townsend, former local representative to the US Congress, was his son in law.

Sale of Pews

The presbyterians raised $20,172 by selling the pews in their new church, on the sale of 52 seats. The highest bid was $750 by S.W. Crosby.

The Black Sheep

There were numerous local failures and bankruptcies. Money was tight. Loans were expected to be scarce come April 1.

Black Sheep were common in those days. Solomon Warner, when he died, left his thriving foundry business east of the Village to two sons. Charley D., the Civil War veteran, in 1872 was showing considerable promise.

The other son, William H., lay in a felon's cell in the Troy jail, under the charge of attempted murder. According to the files of the Old Washington County Post, William was a wild boy from the beginning, restrained until the death of his father. When 21 years old, he was left some Western land and $5,000, a tremendous sum in those days. Had he used the first $5,000 wisely, when his mother died, he would have received another $5,000.

In July, 1871, he turned 21 and received the first $5,000. On 6th St. in Troy one Saturday night in March, 1872, drunk in a house of ill repute, he stabbed his mistress and another harlot.

At the time he received his inheritance, he had been a bartender in Troy, a gay blade and fashion leader. As soon as he got the money he quit his job. He went to Omaha, where his land was. There he met Annie Clark, whom he brought back to Troy. They lived in style until the money ran out.

Then he set out to place Annie in Lena Rivers' whorehouse, which was located off an alley between Broadway and State and 5th and 6th streets. Annie supported him for a time, then she balked.

He became enraged. She slipped away and called a copper. In the presence of the cop, he stabbed both girls. Both survived, but the grand jury indicted him for both stabbings.

In early April, William Warner was released on bail. He married Annie and came to live with Charley in the Village and start a new life.

The year 1872-73 promised to be interesting. Villagers voted 230-59 to issue no liquor licenses. Then the first thing they did to celebrate was get drunk and fire off the old bronze cannon late at night.

The Waite's Corner Hotel was leased from the estate of John Burgess to J.S. Angel.

Colored vs. Irish

That May, Andrew Jackson, a colored porter at the Irving House, who fancied himself a fisticuffer, challenged the house. He announced he could whip any man in the house at 126 lb. or below.

No Irishman could let such a challenge pass. Malachi Shaunessy offered to wrestle Jackson, but finally agreed to box.

They squared off, but Shaunessy clinched and threw Jackson to the saw-dust. They squared off again, and Shaunessy clinched. This time he threw Jackson through the front window of the bar-room.

Jackson went behind the bar and returned to the fray with knife and gun, but was restrained.

William Scranton of Cobbtown was confined in the Saratoga jail for threatening to shoot William Rogers. The disagreement was over a woman. Scranton said he would do it as soon as he was released.

He was also charged for firing the barn of Philo Herrington of the same community, but Scranton said it wasn't him that did it; twas his sister in law.

That June, The Irving House had the only legal bar in the Village, the others having failed to secure licenses under the local option law.

Henry Ackley's pharmacy was licensed to sell medicinal alcohol, but that was challenged by the residents of Town of Cambridge.

The Excise Bd. denied Ackley a medicinal license. Editor Smart warned the temperance people that such an extreme stand would alienate the moderates.

Village have Excise Boards

The Villager of Cambridge Board passed a resolution that April condemning the Town of Cambridge excise board for granting booze licenses within the Village against the wishes of the majority of voters.

Two weeks later, the Governor signed into law a bill forbidding town excise boards from granting booze licenses in incorporated villages. The Villages were to have their own excise boards, composed of the president and two trustees.

Erastus Judson that June resigned from the Village board to avoid serving on the excise bd. He didn't feel that in good conscience he could carry out the wishes of the majority at the recent charter election, when the Villagers voted overwhelmingly to go dry.

Noone wanted to serve on it, although their duty was clear. No booze licenses could be issued.

By July the Village had formed its excise board, the concensus being that no licenses would be issued. However, at its first meeting the Board licensed three hotels, Ira Stroud, C.Ha. Hartt and John Walker. No licenses were given the saloons.

The Village fracas over booze licensing came to a head in October, 1873. The Village President was of the anti-booze group, but the two trustees serving with him on the excise board were elected as license candidates. The Board of Trustees charged the

Excise Bd. to license only the hotels, which they did. However, in late Sept. the McMurray brothers in the West End were granted a license for their saloon. The two pro-license members did it without consulting the third member, the Village President. This week they issued a license to Nicholson and McKie in the East End.

They noted that several petitions had been turned in, requesting the licensing of saloons. They didn't even require the licenses be registered with the Village Clerk.

When the full Board called the pair on their partiality, the wayward trustees, knowing how distasteful was the duty to their colleagues, told the other Trustees that if they did not like it to appoint themselves another Excise Bd.

Beaten to Death

Troy was as tough a city as you found in those days. George W. Smalley of Shushan found this out and the experience that bore the knowledge cost him his life. Smalley lived four days after receiving a fearful beating in the saloon of Michael Doyle, 2nd and Ida Sts., Troy.

John Quinlan and Patrick Maher of Troy were arrested for the crime.

Apparently Quinlan asked Smalley to take a drink with him. Smalley replied that he would not drink with such (remaining censored from the Old WCP). A fight ensued.

Afterwards, Smalley was badly bruised about the body. His eyes were discolored and he had a large bruise on the left temple. He was cut to the bone over the left eye.

An autopsy revealed that he had sustained two skull fractures, both through to the brain. The brain had hemoraged extensively.

The beating supposedly took place outside the saloon, where Doyle supposedly later found Smalley senseless.

Theft & Mayhem

In Murray Hollow that fall, Dave Browner grew tired of living alone. His wife had left him the year before. Browner envied the family of George Fraser, so much that he offered Fraser his horse in a straight swap for Fraser's wife and two kids. Fraser accepted. All parties seemed happy with the deal.

Tommy and Bridget Welch were arrested by Deputy James Archer for stealing various articles from Mrs. Burton Madison. They "were preying upon the people of the Village," wrote the Editor. "Apparently having no home, they are sleeping upon the ground wherever night over-takes them."

Tommy was seven and Bridget ten. Smart found it singular that there was no legal remedy for such a case.

Mayhem reigned that Christmas. Six different brawls stretched the local police force beyond the breaking point. The brawlers were hard-drinking Irishmen in from their tenant farms, celebrating Christmas. Four from Oak Hill took on one officer and anyone who would help him. They couldn't be arrested. One left wearing the handcuffs the officer had snapped on him.

It was sheer mayhem in the now "wet" Village on weekend nights.

In January, 1874, Hiram S. Lee took over management of the Central House from

Hart. And in the Village, the disorder continued unabated. William Mattison, the son in law of the notorious Turnpike murderer Charley Shaw, was arrested for drunkenness, and for possessing a stolen horse and carriage.

A fight in the Irving House resulted when an Englishman, Steward Allen, accused an Irishman, James Boland, of "Popery".

Thomas Christopher and Henry Perry were arrested for the Christmas stabbing of Patrick Hughes. Christopher had to pay Hughes $30, his doctor bills and court costs. The other appeared at another time.

Visitors were allowed poisoner Charley Briggs and his equally guilty paramour, Mrs. Briggs, in their lodgments at the Salem jail **(See Dave' "Murder on the Great Northern Turnpike").**

A new Village Board, "to tempt the never to be found around police" to arrest and confine the disorderly, was to furnish the Lock-up with two bunks and bedding.
That January, 1874 the region was so rowdy that men were hired to walk the tracks to insure the safety of the trains. Early that month once such effort at sabotage was discovered near Cobbtown. Someone had inserted a bridge timber into a cattle guard. The result would have been a derailed train.

In late January, Civil War General Philip Sheridan was a passenger on one of the down cars that passed through the Village.

Editor Smart summed up the depression of the 1870s: "Stagnation in business and a lack of employment everywhere is causing distress and suffering. Cambridge and vicinity is less impacted, but still there are cases that call for aid.

"Able-bodied men go about town seeking work. It is the duty of all men who can afford it to extend the opportunity for employment to the laboring classes, that the sufferings of winter may be lessened."

Failures during the previous two years had dropped out several of the principle local lenders, when Settling Day (April I) came. But money during the day was easy for those with security. Many more mortgagers failed to pay interest and a good deal of foreclosing would follow.

But the depression showed signs of easing. The old WCP reported all tenements filled, whereas at least 30 were vacant a year previous. Prospects for business were also encouraging.

Hugh Cone, hiding out after a fight at the Central House, showed up looking in the worse for wear. He turned himself over to Justice Crocker, who consigned him to the Lock-up.

Patrick Welch was arrested in early April for an assault at the Irving House. It seems he tackled John McNamara, threw him to the floor and bit a piece from his lip.

Cigar Making

Frank McMurray went out of the saloon business, selling his interest in the operation in the basement of Robinson's Store, west of the Union House. McMurray joined B.L. Ward in the cigar making business.

Ben Ward and the McMurray Brothers set up in the new, Harper and McClellan building to manufacture cigars in a big way.

They employed seven and planned to expand to 12.

Minstrel Troupe

The minstrel troupe Clark and Whitmore visited Ackley Hall in early February. Before the show, George Clark complained that one of the pastors discouraged his flock from attending, saying "the Devil would be present".

Clark responded that there was no devil in their show, whatever Devil there was they would take away with them the next day. Possibly we should have had a little Devil; we might have filled a few more seats.

Clark told this story. Supposedly in Manchester, New Hampshire, he faced a lawyer who sought to weaken Clark's deposition by belittling the witness.

He began with a sneer: "You are in the negro minstrel business?

Yes,.

You black your face and sing for a living?

Yes sir.

Well, don't you call that a rather low business?

Well, I don't know but it is, sir; But it is so much better than that of my father before me.

Why. What did your father do?

He was a lawyer.

No further questions.

The life of a minstrel was perilous, at best. life of a minstrel. George, in his act, used a real pistol loaded with powder and paper wadding. Even so, one night its untimely discharge blew off the fore-finger of his right hand.

He would lose the entire arm, eventually, to gangrene infection. It was the beginning of the end for one of the Northeast's most popular vaudevillians.

Temperance Momentum

In 1874, the nation-wide Temperance forces made an effort to regain the momentum the Civil War cost them. The movement was led by women, a further indication of why the Prohibition and Suffrage movements were so intertwined and inseparable.

The national leader was Die Lewis (check spelling, etc.).

The scheme was for the women of a city or village to visit dram sellers and hold prayer meetings in the saloons.

Congressman Smart thought this had the flavor of fanaticism. "But so have all Crusades," he acknowledged. "No friend of the Cause should throw obstacles in the way.

In March, the Village Board notified illegal booze sellers to close shop or face indictment.   In the Village election of the spring, 1874, Temperance was the only issue. The caucus was well attended.

"There were the tee-totalers, your impracticable temperance men and your practicable temperance men; there were those who send up their kegs marked molasses and get them filled with gin; the fellows who preach temperance year round and guzzle on the sly; there were your moderate chaps; the free and easys and the whiskey straights, down to the sore-eyed rummies; some opposed to any license, to those who wanted all licensed. So could get a "Dhrop of the Rale Auld Sthuff."

Time for the caucus was time for the circus to begin.

At this point, James R. McClellan calls for an open vote on the candidates. This was unprecedented, but by it he hoped to further the Temperance cause.

J.W. Eddy would become Village president. That was easily agreed to, but the Temperance forces wanted guarantees. Eddy was a Temperance man, but not a candidate of Mr. McClellan's No License group. They pulled out of the caucus.   But before leaving, James McClellan, James Thompson and R.K. Crocker made impassioned speeches for taking the license question directly to the people. The caucus voted to do this.

The next day the No License people met and called upon Eddy. They asked him if he would be bound by it if the Village voted No License. He said he would be, so they did not put up an opposition candidate.

The caucus candidates carried the election 161-104, with considerable opposition marshalled by the Pro License forces.

The question of licensing was put directly to Village voters, with No License winning by about the same margin, 148-122.

The people voted the usual $500 to operate the Village for a year.

J.W. Eddy was elected Village president, over Thomas Gifford. Trustees J.B. Rice, Albert Tomlinson and William D. Bishop for the West defeated Alfred Worth, George Robertson. Bishop was unopposed.

In the East, Jonathan Dorr Hall, Platt Gilbert and William P. Robertson defeated Alfred Woodworth and W.W. Brockway. Robertson was unopposed. James Thompson was unopposed for Treasurer.

The week after the election, the OLD excise bd. was to meet to issue licenses for the coming year.

The Temperance Women assaulted Battenville that May. Mrs. Dibble, Mrs. McLean and Mrs. Hyatt visited every family in the 'Ville, securing their pledges and "bringing the whiskey men to unconditional surrender".

Greenwich formed a Temperance Union with 600 members to oppose excise licenses. The night before the election, the old board licensed anyone who wanted a license.

To control the Union, the election was held on the third floor of the post office. There were no chairs and lighting was poor. Nonetheless, the Temperance ticket triumphed.

Excise Boards were coming under such heavy attack from women that they had to hide out. The Village Excise Board scheduled a meeting for one Monday night in June, 1874 and a delegation of Temperance women awaited. But the three male board didn't show. After the ladies departed, members Tomlinson and Hall got together at Tomlinson's store and licensed:

S.I. Stroud's Irving House, H.S. Lee's Central House, Henry Ackley's drug store and Mortimer D. Whitcomb's saloon.

The Old WCP criticized the excise board's lack of manliness.

The licenses brought $30 each from the hotels and $10 from the druggist.

Hiram Lee, who had been the landlord for five months, purchased The Central House that June, right after his liquor license was issued.

That June the Governor signed a bill calling for "elected" excise boards at the Town level.

"Path masters" had the responsibility of maintaining roads in the towns. Those who lived along a road could perform a certain amount of work annually, or hire someone to do it for them under the supervision of the Path Master. That June 1874, Laborer William Miller was not working to suit the Path-master Hiram Kenyon in Rd. Dist. # 46. Miller said he was sick.

Kenyon "felt his pulse around the neck", ascertaining that Miller's respiration was very much labored. Miller has since recovered the use of his breathing organs and now works well.

By July, 1874 the courts were tightening the noose on excise violators. Numerous hotel keepers plead guilty and paid fines. In the past, they had escaped the justice of county court since an absurd interpretation, which held that excise violators could not be jailed for failure to appear at the county level. The court of appeals straightened that out and everyone charged started showing up for trial and punishment.

John, the brother of M.D. Hubbard, died in Washington State. He was returned to Cambridge for burial. He had operated a lumber yard where Agway is today, but had sold out a few years previous to Randles and Hall.

In September, 1874 a sparring match was held at Ackley Hall. It was between Sim Watson and Mike Ford of Salem. On the same intertainment bill were clog dancing and horizontal bar exercises.

W.H. Smith and some friends hit town in mid-Sept. He was "looking for his character with a club". They chased Police Justice Leonard Fletcher down Main St. and started after Henry Noble, business manager of the WCP, but could not find him.

Smith was back in town Saturday night, holding forth at one of the hotels, where he got his clothes torn and his eyes blackened.

The Village Police were about to resign en masse because the community has not backed them in trying to stem the recent drunken rioting.

In November the community got rid of one of its worst characters. While James Haggerty, the horse-stealer, was in custody at the Salem Jail, he told the where-abouts of John Cone. Cone was the ring leader of a dreadful riot at the Central House the year before, and had not been apprehended.

Undersheriff William Larmon captured Cone one Saturday night near Galesville (Middle Falls).

"Now the community is in a fair way of getting rid of one of its worst characters," wrote the Post.

Georgie Stewart

George W. Stewart made his first appearance in his hometown since joining the New Orleans Minstrels. They drew well at Ackley Hall in October, 1874. Steward demonstrated his mastery of the Baritone Horn. "His solos on the instrument, which is a difficult one to handle, he exhibited with remarkable talent and cultivation." wrote the WCP reviewer. Stewart would go on to a national reputation, including being one of the founders of the Boston Symphony.

There was also a fine cornet quartette.

Nathan LeBarron was arrested upon suspicion of selling 6,000 lb. or railroad iron to Warner and Green at the foundry. He disappeared right after, and was not seen locally for two years. The day he reappeared, Officer Chappell grabbed him.

Women in Action

In January, 1875 Susan B. Anthony lectured in Shushan on women's suffrage and Temperance.

In February, suits were brought before Police Justice R.K. Crocker against Village hotel and saloon-keepers Ira Stroud, S.I. Stroud, Patrick Gaynor, George Simpson and Mortimer D. Whitcomb.

Mrs. Nancy Wilder signed the complaint. Crocker had forbidden them, under "the act to suppress intemperance, pauperism and crime", to sell booze to her brother, but they did anyway.

Once she got them in court, she told them that while she wasn't afraid of the lot of them, she only brought suit to prevent the future sale of booze to her brother, not to get money out of them. She warned them against future violations, and Justice Crocker let them off with payment of his court cost.

A couple of months later, William Bridgeford had Ira Stroud back in court for selling liquor to a minor, his son.

Miss Mary K. Shiland, a local girl, gave a concert in Ackley Hall. The reviewer thought it good, but "perhaps too classical for the community". She would eventually agree, and move to denver.

Wets Elect Excise Boards

At the spring elections in 1875, the towns of New York State had for the first time the opportunity to vote directly for members of their Excise Boards. Editor Smart thought that Temperance took it on the chin when, out of 17 towns in Washington County, only 10 elected members to Excise Commissions who opposed licensing local establishments.

But given another year under the law, and he predicted that all towns "in the southern assembly district" (south Washington County) would be dry.

However, the three biggest towns went wet, White Creek by 93 votes, Cambridge by 14 and Greenwich by 47.

"We are quite humiliated by this defeat," wrote Editor Smart. "Temperance forces must work harder next year."

But Temperance forces retained a lot of local clout. After winning election on the "pro-license" ticket, Businessman Alfred Worth refused to be sworn as a member for the Town of Cambridge. Another would be sworn only after considerable persuasion.

In anticipation of legal booze sales, the Union House spruced up.

That May the State Attorney General ruled that the new, elected Town excise boards superseded Village excise boards, which were thereby abolished.

Hillman Clan

In April, Constable Clark McClellan found himself in the midst of a Hillman family squabble. Ransom and Henry, both of Jackson, were at odds after Ransom bought Henry's tenant house at a sheriff's sale. Henry assaulted Ransom and was arrested. Then Ransom swore swore a warrant against Henry.

When Constable McClellan went with Ransom to serve the warrant on Henry, they found Henry barricaded inside his house. McClellan kicked in the door and went in with pistol drawn, but Henry knocked him down with a club. With Clark crying to Ransom for help, to no avail, Henry hit him several more times, then fled.

Later McClellan found Henry hiding behind the Bank building, where he meekly surrendered.

Smokers Beware!

Even in 1874 physicians knew smoking was harmful. Their thesis was right, only their science was flawed. One doctor wrote that tobacco smoke interfered with molecular changes coincident with the development of tissues, and made the blood corpuscles oval and irregular at the edge.

Marbles Banned

By-law passed by the Village Board in April. President was J. W. Eddy; Trustees Gilbert, Bishop, Hall, Robertson and Tomlinson:

"All playing of marbles or any game upon sidewalks of this village, thereby obstructing the same, is hereby prohibited, and any person(s) violating said ordinance shall be penalized $1 for the first offense, to $8 maximum fine."

Smart and Noble in April, 1875, bought the lot west of the engine house and planned to break ground May 1 for a building to hold the WCP.

That month, Mattison and Surdam engaged in a "Wild West" shoot-out at Pumpkin Hook.**(See Dave's "Bad Ol' Days", vol. 1.)**

That May, Susan B. Anthony's brother was shot and killed in Leavenworth, Kansas, where he edited the Leavenworth Times. He struck Embury, the editor of the Leavenworth Appeal, and the rival editor shot him fatally through the breast.

Editor Smart thought Anthony always a quarrelsome man.

Albert Welch and Tink Pratt of Cobbtown visited Cambridge Village a Saturday night of late May. After too much "tangle foot", they wandered back up the "Grove". Along the way they overtook Charles LeBarron and Herb Lawrence, whom they soundly beat. Then the pair, perhaps with an augmentation of funds, repaired to Mrs. Riley's "establishment". Despite locked doors and barred windows, they loudly sought entrance. Roused, Mrs. Riley dispatched them with the flat edge of a sword, managing a severe gash in Welch's head.

Observed Robert R. Law, who was then writing for the Old WCP:

"If women could hold office, Mrs. Riley would undoubtedly be the next mayor of Cobbtown". That distinction went to the rowdiest, who seemed to be able to control the rowdies.

Mortimer Whitcomb, who operated a small store and saloon a little east of Dorr's Corners, was issued a store booze license.

After a series of robberies of Village businesses, the businessmen hired a special, night constable.

Recipe for Saratoga Potatoes: Peal good-sized potatoes, slice them as evenly as possible and drop them into ice water. Get a kettle of lard very hot and drop them in a few at a time, stirring until brown.

In the summer of 1875 appeared the announcement that State law required a fire escape on every upper floor hall and business.

In July there was a complaint about "disorderly" houses in the Village.

William AHern that August opened a billiard room over C.H. Robinson's tailor shop.

That November, fire hit the north side of the West End, leveling the Harper and McClellan building, Robinson's building and the Union House.

At the end of 1875 Saloons still operated in the Village. John Morrissey had an establishment under Finn's new Main St. building. John Griffin operated a saloon from part of his harness shop.

The McMurray Brothers, burnt out by the Union House fire, changed businesses again. They bought the soda water business of D.P. Mosher of Eagle Bridge and moved it to Cambridge.

"Charging" Firewood

In April, William "Monarch" Green admitted charging sticks of stove wood with black powder, to discover who was stealing it from him. Michael LeBarron was the indignant thief.

Monarch evidently got the taste for it and would eventually be "charged" with burning a number of his neighbors' barns.

That April, miscreants burned the Village Lock-up. The cubby-hole under the stairs of the engine house was converted for similar temporary use.

In July, 1776, William Laughlin retired "perfectly sober" to his room on the third floor of the Irving House. In the middle of the night he went outside to vomit over the third floor piazza, lost his balance and fell 30 feet to the ground. He was 22 and single. He broke his skull and neck. Two winters previous, his father had frozen to death a couple of miles from the Village.

Walt Hover had been on a tare of some duration, making himself generally disagreeable to the residents of Washington St. On the first Wednesday night in that July he came home drunk and smashed all of his furniture, broke the stove and beat his wife with a fence picket. She escaped with her life to the neighbors.

Prof. Al Hawyer showed up to stop the fight and Hover hit him several times, threatening permanent surgical procedures if the pedant didn't mind his own business.

When several other neighbors joined in with an officer of the law, Hover decamped with his wife's clothes. Constable Howe caught him a week later. He was held for the grand jury under a $250 bond and a peace bond toward his wife of $100.

"Four months in Albany would do him good," concluded the Old WCP.

Family Comstock

The Referee in the J.D. Hall suit against M.D. Hubbard found in favor of Hall. Hall and Randles bought the lumber businesses of M.C. Hubbard and of one jointly held between M.D. and John. When John died out west, M.D. was the executor of his estate. Apparently, Hall didn't feel he was getting all that was due him from the business sale of some years before.

Thomas Comstock was born in Cambridge May 22, 1799. He died at his Village home Jan. 18, 1877. He was descended from a Puritan family. His Grand-father, an officer in the Revolutionary War, was killed at the Battle of Walloomsac (Bennington). His mother was always honored in those early White Creek "Battle Days" parades.

Comstock went to sea at the age of 21, signing on for two voyages of 3 years each. He spent one winter at Nantucket Island.

He was converted by the "silver-tongued" Rev. John N. Moffat, a Methodist minister, since defrocked.

Comstock left the sea for business in Albany, which he continued until 1841, when he returned to Cambridge.

The oldest of three children, he had to provide for the entire family. His mother lived to be 88.

In Albany, Comstock married Phoebe Fowler, the daughter of Thomas Fowler, an early resident of Town of Cambridge.

He was a director of the CV Bank.

One of his peculiarities was his promptness in meeting engagements. His watch was for years the Regulator of the Village.

That January, Whitmore and Clark's Minstrels appeared at Ackley's Hall.

Coila Cornet Band

In February, the old hall in Coila, which had been used years before during a schism in the church, was refitted and opened to the Coila Band.

Rice had replaced Hall with Randles in the lumber business. In February, Randles retired and left it to Rice to carry on.

That February, Dr. Henry Gray died. He was the second great and beloved physician in the history of the community. The first was Dr. Jonathan Dorr, whose practice Gray succeeded to.

Mort Whitcomb

In March, 1877 the rum and cheap whiskey was getting the best of Mortimer Whitcomb. He ran a store and saloon in the East End.
He was brought before the Grand Jury to answer charges of selling booze without an excise license. He appeared drunk, with his clerk, Michael Boland, in support.

When he returned to Cambridge, he found that his wife, one of the daughters of the notorious Charley Shaw, and Boland had locked him out.

Mortimer attracted a crowd of 30-40 to watch him stone his own house with frozen mud and rocks and attempt to kick in his front door.

He was found guilty and fined $50. But being broke, he was confined to the Sheriff's farm until he had worked it off.

Later, he would close out his whiskey business, but continue to sell ale and cider.

Times remained hard. That April, 1877 found few mortgage sales on Settling Day. Farmers had gotten high prices for what few potatoes had gotten past the potato and "chintz" bug, both new to the area. There were few farm bankruptcies, because of the disinclination of the mortagagee to take the land, not because of easing times.

George Pratt turned State's evidence on Surdam and Mattison, who had shot it out that winter at Pumpkin Hook. The result was that he and they received one year at hard labor at the county jail, for petit larceny.

That April, George Law began to erect a $30,000 home at what would be called "Content Farm". Today that mansion would cost more like $1 million plus to raise.

An early barrister, H.K. Sharpe, died that April. He had long suffered from consumption.

Drunken Rape

In May, excessive drinking led to a terrible crime on the Ashgrove Rd. Mrs. Margaret Monroe, a widow, lived with two small children a mile east of the Village.

Four drunks hired Ike Mattison to take them to the widow's door. There they proceeded to kick it in. They threw her to the floor and, while the others held her, took turns raping her.

Two passing strangers heard her screams, stopped and looked, but did not dare to interfere. The "party" was broken up when
her son arrived.

The men fled into the Grove toward Vermont. Patrick Jones and Peter Matthews were later captured, but the others were never found. Jones and Matthews were held for the Grand Jury, in lieu of $2,000 bond each.

In August, Kate Whaley appeared before Police Justice Mooney on a complaint of prostitution. Complainant did not appear, so the judge told her to leave town.

In September, St. Luke's got a new bell, cast in Troy.
"Uncle Tom's Cabin" played at Ackley's Hall to a small crowd.

Crystal Palace Arson
In late September, fire erupted in S.B. Hall's "Crystal Palace" saloon. It was located in the basement of Finn's new building, which had been constructed beside C.S. Robinson's building and tailor shop, west of Rice's seed rooms, which were at that time west of the Union House.

Finn was operating a wagon shop. Arson was suspected.

The "Crystal Palace" had recently been the scene of a Western-style shoot-out, so it is likely that Temperance forces burned him out.

Hall next leased "The Old Red Grocery" on the Arlington Highway. This historic farm had at one time belonged to a "Loyalist", Carcallan, in those turbulent times prior to the Revolutionary War. The family was forced to flee to Canada and the farm was given as a reward to a "patriot".

Since then it had served as an inn and stage-coach stop on the run out of Vermont. Hall proposed to escape the watchful eye of the Temperance folk, while stocking the grocery "with liquid refreshments".

In April, 1878, The Red Grocery burned, together with all of its out-buildings. The former keeper of "The Crystal Palace" seemed to have many enemies.

In October, Ira Stroud sold the lot where the old Union House had burned to Perry Eldred of Hoosick Falls for $6,000. Eldred would build the famous version.

Citizens of the Village pledged $1,250 toward the purchase, on the promise that a first class hotel would be built there.

"Bucky" Priest
On September 27th, one William Priest of Shushan married Jennie Barnes. A week later, he was forcibly taken from his bride's father's house "by local malcontents and rowdies and for reasons unknown," tarred and feathered.**(See Dave's "A Poisoned Romance at Eagleville".)**

Times continued hard in the 1870's. The fledgling Greenwich and Johnsonville Railroad, in 1877, was unable to meet its obligations to investors. They blamed a general stagnation of business, but hoped to make interest payments when the next coupons matured.

Horse Thieves
In November, Deputy Sheriff James Archer broke up a ring of horse and harness

thieves, tracking them to their lairs across the Northeast. Chris Shaw, son of the notorious poisoner Charley Shaw, was found holed up near Boston. Mary J. Shaw was found in Schuylerville. Their partners, Frank and Dennis Pratt, were found in Annaquasicoke and White Creek. Fred Lamphier was caught in Saratoga.

Dennis Pratt was "lodged in our model lock-up". Since the original lock-up had been burned by rowdies, the Village had made do with the cubby-hole under the stairs in the aging Engine House.

Archer Placed Pratt in there hand-cuffed. But between 1 and 3 a.m. he escaped. He made a hook from the bail of the "thunder mug" and with it, started a board from the ceiling. The rest was easy.

Winter entertainments drew poorly behaved crowd. In Ackley's Hall, "a rabble" had the habit of hanging around outside the entrance and harassing those with tickets. This poor, often drunken "rabble" drew its entertainment from the well-dressed gentry and their nicely appointed carriages that drew them to the step in front of Ackley's Hall. The WCP wanted a policeman in attendance to secure order.

On the 28th of December, 1877, the Whitmore and Clark Minstrel troupe returned to Ackley Hall.

In that same issue of the Old WCP it was announced that M.D. Hubbard would build a new hall between his storehouse and the Bank.

Murphy Movement

As the year 1878 dawned, the "Murphy" movement swept the community. It sought to unite all men of different degrees of Temperance against the common enemy.

Francis Murphy was an outstanding orator of the time. His assistant, Col. Caldwell, spoke in Greenwich early in January and was due a week later at the ME Church in Cambridge.

Editor Smart did not care for the movement. He felt that the object of Murphy's "Blue Ribbon" movement was too single-minded, to pursuade the individual to practice total abstinence, rather than to get Temperance forces to vote as a block.

Smart thought that the sale of liquor would not be stemmed by such a movement, but rather by the actions of individuals.

At the annual spring elections, a "no license" excise board was put in place in White Creek, but "license" forces prevailed in Cambridge.

That May a schism surfaced in the Temperance movement. Some wanted to throw out the old leaders for not being severe enough with those who couldn't hold to their pledges. The Post chided these "perfect men" and called for more Christian charity toward all.

In the meantime, the White Creek Excise Board met and granted no licenses at all.

By June, the Temperance flap was quite hot. In a meeting at Fuller's Hall, Leonard Fletcher resigned as chairman. James R. McClellan was elected.

This is sadly ironic, for but a few years hence, Leonard Fletcher, local attorney, police judge and manager of the Stars baseball club, would die under the cars, a confirmed alcoholic.

McClellan, on the other hand, had to watch his boy carted away to prison for a crime he committed while drunk.

The entire Temperance executive committee resigned with Fletcher. Rev. Mooney moved the resignations be accepted.

James S. Smart rose to speak in their behalf. He reminded the gathering of the Murphy Pledge, which promised "Malice toward none, charity for all".

None the less, E.P. Cramer moved that a new committee be elected. There was a long, embarrassed silence, followed by a second. But then the democratic process broke down into arguments well off the subject.

Noone wanted to be elected to the new committee. Dr. B.F. Ketchum rose to speak. He admitted throwing a "brickbat" at the previous meeting. He agreed that the Temperance society should show charity toward the fallen, but protested that they should not be the leaders. This was probably an allusion to Lennie Fletcher.

Ketchum noted that Smart would occasionally lift a dram, despite his pledge.

Smart protested that he had joined the Murphy movement at the urging of a woman who felt his example might stimulate her husband to control his drinking.

Whereupon, Editor Smart resigned and renounced his pledge.

Rev. Blinn, who would be catalyst in one of the worst splits in local church history, rose to announce that such lay endeavors were doomed to die of discord; and that such a movement belonged within the church.

Without waiting for formal adjournment, the meeting sort of dispersed with Editor Smart.

"So," concluded the ever present WCP scribe, "With this not very pleasant after-piece, we ring down the curtain on the Cambridge Temperance Union".

Hat-pin Defense

Several ladies were insulted by drunks on the Village streets that June. One woman was accosted by a drunk who stepped out from between two buildings and clasped her by the elbow. But the lady was ready for him. Ladies who had to be about on the Village streets of the evening had long learned the defensive efficacy of the hat pin. Hers was ready and she drove it to the hilt in the villain's arm.

With the ever-present danger of death from blood poisoning, the ladies hat pin gave more than one ne'er do well pause when tempted to assault one of the "weaker sex".

That March, "Texas Jack" appeared on the stage of Ackley's Hall. His dramatization of "Life on the Frontier" included feats of marksmanship by "a celebrated pigeon shooter".

In July Harry O. Barton, while drunk, took after his wife with a knife and succeeded in cutting down the clothes line. He was a peaceful man when sober.

On August 16, 1878 W.H. Reed, the proprietor of the hotel at White Creek Center, held a Battle of White Creek (or Walloomsac, or Bennington) dance.

Long before there was a Great Cambridge Fair, there was a driving park on the Sanderson Farm, called The Cambridge Driving Park.

That September, 1878, the talk of the corporation was a plan to enlist Martin Rice as the fire alarm, with William Stover as his second. It seems that when the pair got drunk, their bellowing awakened the entire Village.

Firehouse Makes Way

The Village Board, led by new President James Ellis, voted to move the Engine House out of the way of Pearl St. and to build a lock-up underneath.

Wm. P. Robertson, Trustee, resigned from the Lock-up Committee, as he had sought a fire-proof just east of the fire house.

The Town of White Creek Excise Board, which had issued no licenses the year 1878, warned violators to expect prosecution. At the Baptist Church a Temperance group formed to help enforce the excise law.

That September, the Village Board contracted with William Livingston to move the fire house east onto a lot which was deeded to the Village by Jerome B. Rice. Rice wanted Pearl St. extended south of Main St. to solve an entrance problem into the swampland he had bought from Robert Blair and was converting to his seed company home grounds.

It was moved in early October. A "Mr. Hoag" did it, using a horse, a windlass and stakes driven into the ground.

The 1880s

As the 1880s approached, the community seemed to come back to life. Booze seemed to be under some control through the Town excise boards. Immigration was taking West all who weren't tied to local success or responsibility. As the '80s dawned, there was a feeling of opportunities opening.

The Peck Bros. leased the Irving House for another year that April I. They would eventually become local coal suppliers.

Dennis Tracy, that April 1, purchased the old Loomis Block (Hitchcock).

That May, the Town of Cambridge Excise Board issued two booze licenses. The licenses, $50 each, went to druggists D. M. Smith and Decker and Co.

As of that May, the White Creek Board had issued no licenses.

But for the Post Editor, it still wasn't enough control. "This makes 12 licensed places in the Village," he observed, "Besides the unlicensed." Evidently White Creek did not make good on its threat to crack down on illegal booze sellers.

Poor Mortimer Whitcomb was arrested on a bench warrant, at the insistance of his wife, and was put under a bond to keep the peace. Mortimer's problems were blamed in the consumption of liquor.

But Whitcomb couldn't control his month-long spree. He surrendered his bond and was sent to Salem jail.

Ordinarily an abstainer, the Post reported he had been drinking heavily. Justice R.K. Crocker committed him after he voluntarily submitted in order to break his "spree".

Cobbtown Conspiracy

In January, 1880, Deputy Sheriff James Archer was investigating the recent burglaries of Joe Paro's tailor shop and Carpenter's Jewelry Shop, both located between Hubbard's Hall and the railroad.

As the Christmas Eve theft also involved the loss of some harnesses at T.E. Beebe's business in Shushan, suspicion naturally fell upon the denizens of Cobbtown.

Michael LeBarron had been seen around in the company of Mrs. Bentley. Archer found men's suits taken from Paro's shop in the Bentley house. Also found there were items taken from B.F. McNitt's store in a heist back in October, 1879.

On his way into Cambridge with his buck-board loaded with stolen goods, Archer met the Griffin boys, Gideon and John. As LeBarron and Bentley had implicated them, he arrested both and drove with them back to Cambridge.

Carpenter identified several articles from his shop, spectacles, two watches, and a fruit knife carried by the Griffin boys.

Archer saw the boys duly arrested and held. Then started for the LeBarrons back in Cobbtown. He found Michael in bed asleep, fully clothed, except for his boots.

When arrested, both LeBarrons and the Griffin boys were wearing clothes stolen from McNitt. All were indicted by the Grand Jury.

Editor Smart wanted more funds to be allotted to Archer so that he could "get at the entire LeBarron gang." It seems that in those day, any investigative work was done at the expense of the officer, unless he was compensated by the victims.

Booze Gets Blood

Booze still flowed. In late March, Eben Ross started home to White Creek after a Saturday of drinking. He fell from his wagon and broke his neck. He left a family.

In May, 1880, the Poormaster of the Town of Cambridge, on the complaint of White Creek citizens, sued two saloon keepers, Jack Morrissey and James Finn of Cambridge, for violation of the excise law. Finn paid $50 and costs, Morrissey $100.

The O'Sheas of Blind Buck Hollow were heavy drinkers. Catherine O'Shea went to Salem on a Tuesday night in June, 1880, returning home on Wednesday. When she did, husband James beat her.

Thursday morning she was sufficiently recovered to report as usual to Levi Copelands to help with the milking.James O"Shea came after her and that was the last time she was seen alive.

She was found in the livingroom of the O'Shea tenement, her blood splattered over the walls and floors. She had been beaten and stabbed repeatedly. A severe blow to the back of the head killed her.

Husband James said that she fell down the stairs, although the stairs were one of the few areas not spattered with her blood.

The coroner's jury concluded that Catherine had been murdered by James; that he had assaulted her both Wednesday and Thursday nights; and that "rum was the occasion of all the difficulties".

In July of 1880 the Board of Health passed a resolution forbidding church funerals over anyone who died of diphtheria or any other contagious disease.

In December, 1880, Andrew B. McNish and Henry Billings bought the Hurd & Co. Store, in the Hubbard Block, and opened for business. Evidently the first occupant of the double store under the hall was Hurd & Co.

In March, 1881, the famed portrayer Joseph Jefferson played the title role in "Rip Van Winkle" at Hubbard's Hall.

In May, 1881 the Town of White Creek Excise Board granted licenses to H.S. Lee of the Central House, Potter of the Irving House, Acker Houghton of the Fenton House and W.H. Reid of White Creek Village.

In Cambridge Village, saloons licensed were operated by Frank McMurray, Dennis Tracey and Mortimer Whitcomb.

Hotels paid $30 for a liquor license. Saloons paid $10 for an ale license.

The Town of Cambridge Excise Board granted only medicinal drug store licenses, to Dr. D.M. Smith and R.J.C. Williams, at $10 each.

In September, 1881 the third annual county Civil War Veterans Reunion was held at Argyle. It wasn't what many expected. Baxter's Hotel (the only one) provided ample housing and plenty of iced water. They weren't particularly liberal in the way of drinks, the Post correspondent reported. In fact, except for the bootlegging of substances that looked a lot like birch beer or raspberry syrup, which the correspondent thought were quite potent, the affair was "dry".

Those veterans that got drunk brought the bottles with them. Town of Argyle was dry then and was still dry in 2010.

Plethora of Grog Shops

In December, 1881 DENNIS PLUNKETT'S EAST END BAR IN THE FORMER LIVERY STABLE OF A. FOWLER RECEIVED THE OLD BAR SAVED FROM THE BURNED WHITE CREEK HOTEL.

An estimate by the Old WCP of the number of "grog shops" operating within the Village that summer of 1882 was 14, one for every 100 residents.

Citzens presented petitions to the White Creek Excise Board asking them not to license saloons, but the Board would not listen.   Prohibition was long over-due.

In November, 1885 the new Union House opened. The Cambridge House had won the race, throwing open its doors a few weeks earlier.

That same November, residents gathered in Hubbard's Hall to form a "Law and Order League" to enforce the liquor license law in the Village, something the Village Board hadn't the stomach to undertake.

Thomas Gifford was elected chairman. The group visited each liquor seller and called his attention to the law. They were treated civilly except by one "O'Brien" at the old Fenton House.

That is the establishment "Al" Herrington was going to make into a model hotel. O'Brien would not give them access.

The result was that everyone (except O'Brien, of course) refrained from selling booze on Sunday.

A Hot Coincidence

It was perhaps but coincidence that five days after the "Law and Order" piece appeared in the Old WCP, both of A.A. Herrington's establishments on East Main St. went up in smoke and flames.

One was the historic tavern on the corner of S. Park and E. Main St., managed by O'Brien.

The one next to it was occupied by Frank Kennedy as a saloon.

O'Brien's hotel was thought to have been built in 1795, and may have been the second hotel on the site. Woods' Tavern would have been earlier.

Adonijah Skinner kept it after 1795. He added a second floor for Masonic rooms, perhaps the first in the community.

Major John Porter succeeded Skinner. He kept it until 1815, when it became the Widow Comstock's Tavern. Later Zal Fenton kept it.

Observed the unbending Editor of the Old WCP: "No worse places were kept in the Village than by Kennedy and O'Brien".

At the end of 1885, "The Law and Order League" wore one arrest and prosecution on their belts, not counting the two arsons. They continued to meet at Hubbard's Hall. Five hundred attended their May meeting. The Temperance movement was well under way. H. R. Eldridge was president, but the driving force was the local ministers.

The winter of 1887, the Temperance effort was redoubled. All of the ministers preached temperance sermons on Sunday, then on Monday night there was a mass Temperance meeting at Hubbard's Hall.

The "Local Option" feature of the Excise Law of that time posed serious problems to the local Inns. The spring of 1888, Cambridge issued a license to the Union House, but White Creek went "dry", meaning that the The Irving House and The Cambridge House couldn't sell booze, while the Union House could. It put the proprietors at a decided disadvantage in competing for the trade. As one might expect, D.C. Stroud of the Irving House ignored the law and paid a $50 fine, rather than lose the trade.

In the summer of 1893, the Temperance movement was so strong that even the venerable Dr. Henry Blackfan was not above prosecution. The genial proprietor of Lauderdale House was arrested and charged with selling alcoholic beverages without a license. His bail was $325. It seems that some guests saw ale in the possession of other guests and wanted some. James Weir, who was also charged, procured four bottles for them.

The charge was eventually dropped.

Temperance was giving way to Abstinence; Mr. Rockwell, as of January, 1895 ceased to sell liquor at the Union House.

Booze Sales Built
Cambridge Town Hall

Taking advantage of the new excise laws, the voters of Town of Cambridge voted 61-3 to accept money from the excise and to use $1,100 of it to erect a town hall.

Apparently the only reason the community had tolerated the venerable and often disreputable Center Cambridge Hotel was that it was the only hall suitable for public meetings.

The contract went to A.J. Eycleshymer of Cambridge Village for $1,074. Horace Dodds lost out with a bid of $1,200. McCrea Hedges bid $1,250.

The hall progressed rapidly. It was described in mid-September:

It was going up on the south side of the street "at the junction with the Greenwich road". Dimensions were 30 x 55 ft. The floors were of Georgia pine. The hall had a 14 ft. ceiling.The stage was 14 ft wide and l0 deep. On either side were to be small 'tiring rooms. It had double windows and a basement in the rear for fuel storage.

The lot was 90 ft. on the highway and 120 ft. deep. (In those days), the building was 15 ft from the road, with 30 ft. of space on either side and 50 ft. in the rear. Behind the hall, 20 ft. would be used for a shed or carriage barn to be constructed in the future.

The site being on gravelly, slightly inclined ground, mire would be minimized.

In February, 1898 the Hall was ready for its first public use, the Republican caucus.

Quoth Editor Smart, himself a Cambridge Republican, although prone to break away from the dogma: "It will be a luxury to have so spacious and convenient a hall for this, after the many years of the great inconvenience to which the voters have been subjected by the dingy and narrow accommodations of the old basement".

This despite the fact that taxes raised by the sale of liquor had built it.

The fate of the old Center Cambridge Hotel had been sealed when it was struck off in foreclosure auction to its neighbor, Fred Ingraham, for $330.

After the construction of the Greenwich and Johnsonville RR, little custom came its way from the drovers and draysmen that once stopped there, for it had been a stop for freighters between Greenwich and Buskirk's Bridge.

Its liquor sales were viewed by locals as a nuisance, at the least. There was worry in the community that it would be reopened for that traffic.

Most of the Raines Law revenues that built the new, Town Hall came from the Union House and saloons on the West End of Cambridge Village. There was always the possibility that someone like the Fisher family, who had been driven away, would start up that traffic again.

But its sale to Mr. Ingraham, a righteous and moral industrialist and farmer, put an end to that concern.

But many a local had attended balls there. The "spring floor" under the ballroom was still good, although the horse sheds had rotted away. A room just north of the hotel had been rented as a storehouse.

But generally, the place was a wreck.

A preacher, holding forth in the nearby schoolhouse (now a private home) had called it "the old, red, hell-hole."

In 1898 Charles Anson Ingraham, minister, author and son of Frederick, recalled its history.

It had seen much use for community gatherings, whether town meetings or dances. Jesse Wood, the first Center Cambridge boy to die in the Civil War, was laid out there, taken from the pine shipping box and given a suitable burial.

A multitude of elections had been held in the ballroom. One of the wildest, according to Ingraham, was a special meeting held during the Civil War to decide if soldier votes were to count. The day was rainy and the vote light, so one of the inspectors tuned up his fiddle and the day was spent in dancing something the Editor called "The French Four".

Martin I. Townsend, a favorite U.S. Representative, who had married a Cambridge girl, was sure to appear there during the political season. Townsend spoke to a large crowd, in favor of Lincoln, during his reelection campaign, his opponent being Gen.

McClellan.

"While Martin was waxing eloquent, democrat voices were heard from outside, shouting, "Mac!, Mac!, Mac!" Townsend was equal to the heckling.

"It reminds me of the time," he said, "When an Irish peddler who went through the streets of Troy crying 'Fresh mackeral!' A man stopped him, and while inspecting his wares, smelled of one.

'Why man,' sez he, 'your fish are not fresh; smell of them!'
The peddler took one whiff and picking up his reins hurried away, calling, 'Fresh mac, mac, mac!'

"His fish were so strong he couldn't utter another syllable."

"It was only a question of time," wrote Charles A. Ingraham, "Before the old hotel and its broken backed barn would fall, the foundation stones thrown down and the plow and the scraper shall do their work of obliteration.

"Then shall the virgin grass spring on the place of revelry and all the people say 'Amen!'"

McMurray's "Hotel"

McMurray, in May, 1897, built a Raines "hotel" on the corner of N. Union and Main St. According to the new excise law, to qualify for a booze license, it had to be a hotel with a minimum number of rooms. Nothing was said of the size of rooms or if they were used.

This building would replace the old storehouse of Leonard Wells, which had been moved to the site from south of the Village, and which had burned the previous year.

Julius Moeller's barber shop was moved from the McMurray lot across the street south (to where IGA was in 2010).

McMurray's "hotel" opened with 100 in attendance at the free lunch. The "handsome bar was easily seen from the street".

Half a barrel of clams had been set aside for the chowder, but having other things on their minds, the boys failed to ice them and had to do with beef soup.

That August, 1898, McMurray's hotel had "tasty" signs painted on its windows.

That fall, a "couche-couche" show opened at the Fair. Hon. D.M. Westfall represented the Village in prosecuting the owner.

But it wasn't so easy to push around these "carnie:" types.
The owner threatened the Fair officers with a liability suit, they spoke to the Village Board and the show (no doubt with a few more "pasties" in place) went on.

This would not pass unnoticed. The next Sunday, Rev. Turnbull preached a blistering sermon. He indicted the Village Board for its failure to control the drunken rabble which the Fair attracted, in what he characterized as "the annual disturbance and disgrace for our Village".

In October, 1898, the annual, County WCTU convention was held in Hubbard's Hall.

A prohibition meeting in the Hall in November was well attended. The Prohibition Party was then running candidates for public office. Coila Pastor Rev. J.C. Scott introduced the candidate for Sec. of State, Henry Wilbur, who made a "plain speech for over an hour and possibly won the vote of a few 'doubting' Republicans". The Democrats, to hear Editor Smart tell it, were for no license requirements and wide open saloons.

However trivial it might seem to the major parties, the Prohibition ticket that election day polled 7 votes in Cambridge, 29 in White Creek and 15 in Jackson. Who at that time could foresee the day when the Prohibition Party would shut down the booze halls of the Nation?

Hubbard Hall was used considerably as the community went through its periodic convulsion in attempting to shut down the saloons.

After a day of caucusing on the Prohibition question, weary citizens gathered at Scott's infamous "Raines hotel" (East End) "for restful recreation after the setting sun had proclaimed...," etc.

By 9 p.m. the denizens were beginning to respond to the gentle ministrations of Scott's home-made lager and cheap whiskey. Tom Mooney received several gashes on the head from a spittoon, which attacked him without provocation.

It also drove out the big window at the front.

The landlord himself had the meat stripped from one thumb by the teeth of an ungracious guest, who declined to be separated of his off eye.

Wrote Editor James Stevenson Smart --- a former captain of artillery in the Civil War: "Now who will have the heart to vote out of existence places so conducive to the refreshment of our weary and less opulent citizens?"

Under the Raines Law, Scott paid a $200 annual license fee to operate as a "hotel". That fee was totally returned to the Town government, which, as editor Smart feared, created an atmosphere of toleration for the intolerable.

The following week, Scott, the inn keeper, wrote a letter in defense of his establishment.

Was this the only fight on caucus day, he asked?

"There were three rows, almost within a stones throw of each other."

His defense continued: "It is the fault of the rich citizens, who buy votes of the poor boys, thereby providing them the wherewithal".

With unerring logic, he concludes: "Knowing how the money will be used, who is responsible for the result?"

Perhaps it is not surprising that in that election, "White Creek" stayed "wet".

Checking the "Evil"

But there were ways to keep the forces of evil in check, other than at the ballot box. Early Friday morning, the 22nd of April Scott's Raines Hotel went up in smoke and flames, taking with it Nicholson's Hardware and Hitchcock's Haberdashery. This burned off the section of Cambridge Village which is known today as The Hitchcock Block.

Proprietor Scott complained that when he arrived at the scene he found that front door of his saloon was broken in, but there is no record of an investigation.

By May, Hitchcock had purchased the neighboring Tracy lot and began to erect the present brick block. Nicholson cleared away the ruins of his brick veneer structure to erect a two story brick building, which stands to this day.

The ruins of the Scott Raines hotel was cleared away, to make way for another one. Scott built it two stories high, but crowded in three floors in order to provide the number of "cribs" required under the Raines law.

The new Raines Hotel was ready by fair time. The newly organized, "Good Citizens League" tried to block the relicensing, but the County Treasurer issued a license, anyway, to Proprietor John H. Scott. A year later the State Court of Appeals agreed, calling the fire "a temporary halt in business". No new license was required.

Today the old, wooden Raines hotel stands directly west of the new brick building Nicholson put up by Hitchcock's new Block.

It is located west of the Hitchcock Block and immediately west of what old-timers will remember as Sam Weller's Café (home of fried donuts and home-made pie).

Since its days as a Raines Hotel, the building has served as Santerre's Liquor Store and a nickel and dime store. In 2010 it served as residence apartments.

The Good Citizens League set out to put Scott's Raines hotel out of business for good. They failed to keep him from getting a hotel booze license. But Frank Larmon was a brand-new engineer from RPI. He measured the distance between Scott's and the Congregational Church (where A & M Printers is today) and discovered that it was less than 200 ft., the distance required by law between a house of worship and a booze hall. By Larmon's measure, 199 ft., 6 inches separated the two buildings.

But Scott's wasn't the only Raines hotel in the East End. Frank Plunkett operated one near Beach's Hall (where Rite Aid is today).

It was a tough way to make a buck, running a hotel. Frank McMurray, lessee of the Irving House, "decamped" right after the Cambridge Fair closed one September, "leaving behind a number of creditors to regret their brief acquaintance with him".

McMurray had leased "on promises" that Augus, just in time for the fair, and had bought the contents of the bar from the hotel owner, D.C. Stroud. He promised installments would be paid during fair week, when the Village over-flowed with thousands of visitors.

The bar trade was great! The stock reduced, the expectant Stroud replenished it.

McMurray was a likable guy. Local businessmen supplied him "on tick". Three Albany brewers lent him $150 each to get started.

But the first (and only) check McMurray wrote Mr. Stroud was for $100 on a Vermont bank "of questionable worth".

When Stroud pressed him, McMurray showed Stroud a thick roll and dared him to try to get it.

That same night, McMurray packed and left on the down train, destination unknown.

Of course, the Vermont check was no good and Stroud was out $1,000.

The Irving House was a huge pile of bricks located at Main and Park Sts. where Cumberland Farms is today. It was built sometime in the 1840s and enjoyed very few prosperous years before it was demolished 110 yrs. later.

News-Maker

The year 1902 was no exception for the Irving House, in terms of profitability, because it didn't have a booze license in 1902, either.

But Frank Plunkett did. He operated a saloon a few rods east of Beach's Hall. That whole corner was cleared when they built the new A & P (now Rite Aid).

For a saloon operator, Plunkett was a great news-maker. One day in March, 1902 he strode across the street from his Raines Hotel and punched young Weston Mitchell in the face.

Mitchell and some other young "toughs" were sitting on Joe Paro's new fence in front of Paro's house, which he had just recently painted dark green. Paro had built the big Victorian that still sits on the southeast corner of the Broad and Main St. intersection. Plunkett thought the boys were talking about him.

Mitchell got even by testifying that Plunkett had served him booze on Sunday, but with local legal ace Eliot Norton defending him, Plunkett got off with the $20 fine for assault.

Brought to Bear

Once the operator of a rum hole made the pages of the Old Washington County Post, the forces of Temperance were brought to bear. A neighbor complained that the door to Plunkett's saloon was too close to his residence.

Men of the Cambridge Prohibition Alliance measured the distance and found to the satisfaction of the law that Plunkett's saloon door was, indeed, five feet too close to his neighbor's domicile.

There is about Old Cambridge denizens something of the Rebel, the outcast, the renegade.

We fought the Yorkers in 1763 and we fought the Brits ten years later. We don't like conservation officers, who criticize us for shooting a little table meat. We like our beautiful valleys, but we don't want to be told not to drain our toilets and used crank case oil into the brook, or not to burn our leaves or to pay $2 a bag for the privilege of letting someone else burn our garbage.

We don't like a whole lot of Government and we always pull for the little guy, even if he is a saloon keeper.

The way Plunkett found his way out the of the legal maze the "dries" had caught him in has made him something of a local folk hero to this day.

Instead of closing his business and sneaking out of town, he "borrowed" some planks from a less than vigilant neighbor and boarded up the offending door. Then he cut a door hole at the other end of the building.

It is perhaps because of our rebellious natures and our natural distaste for regulation and control that it was 1888
before the Village got serious about controlling its saloons.

That May, the Village took the first dramatic step to control the run-away saloons operating on Main St. The vote was to prosecute those selling booze "on Sunday" without a license.

Editor Smart thought it a step in the right direction, but suggested the phrase "on Sunday" be left out.

"The growth in number of saloons in this Village in recent years is astounding," he noted.

Law & Order League

November of that same year, residents gathered in Hubbard's Hall to form a "Law and Order League" to enforce the liquor license law in the Village, something the Village Board hadn't the stomach to undertake.

Thomas Gifford was elected chairman. The group visited each liquor seller and called his attention to the law.

They were treated civilly except by one "O'Brien" at the old Fenton House. It stood on the south corner of Main and Park, where the Cambridge Floral Shop is today. It and a "billiard Parlor" next door were owned by A.A. Herrington.

O'Brien would not give them access.

The result was that every saloon keeper, except O'Brien, refrained from selling booze on Sunday.

It is perhaps but coincidence that five days after the "Law and Order" piece appeared in the Old WCP, both of A.A. Herrington's establishments on East Main St. went up in smoke and flames.

One was the historic tavern on the corner of S. Park and E. Main St., managed by O'Brien, the site upon which Paro would build.

The "billiard parlor" next to it was really occupied by Frank Kennedy as a saloon.

O'Brien's building had been built in 1795, and may have been the second hotel on the site, Woods' Tavern having been earlier.

Adonijah Skinner had kept it after 1795. He added a second floor for Masonic rooms.

Major John Porter succeeded Skinner. He kept it until 1815, when it became the Widow Comstock's Tavern. Later Zal Fenton kept it.

That an historic building was lost and one drunken soul incinerated in the blaze in no way daunted the unbending Editor of the Old WCP.

"No worse places were kept in the Village than by Kennedy and O'Brien," was his epitaph.

Even the venerable Dr. Henry Blackfan was not above prosecution. The genial proprietor of Lauderdale House, at the north end of the lake by that name, was arrested and charged with selling alcoholic beverages without a license. His bail was $325. It seems that some guests saw ale in the possession of other guests and wanted some. James Weir, who was also charged, procured four bottles for them.

The charge was eventually dropped.

By then the Law and Order League had a few "scalps" on their belts. Their regular meetings at Hubbard's Hall were well attended, five hundred in May.

Temperance Movement

The old Temperance movement had not lost its fire, either.
H. R. Eldridge was its president, but the driving force, of course, were the local ministers.

The "Local Option" feature of the Excise Law of that time posed serious problems for the Inns, as they competed for the same custom, but existed in separate towns. Two towns ---Cambridge and White Creek --- bisect the Village of Cambridge, with the Town of Jackson touching on the north.

For example, one spring, Cambridge might issue a license to the Union House, which was in the Town of Cambridge; but White Creek might be "dry", meaning that the Irving House and The Cambridge House couldn't sell booze. It put the proprietors at a decided disadvantage in competing for the trade.

As one might have anticipated, D.C. Stroud, while owner of the Irving House, ignored the law and paid his $50 fines, rather than lose the trade.

But by April, 1902, after Stroud had died and David Turner managed the Irving House for his estate, things were tougher for the booze merchant.

Turner wasn't let off with just a fine. He was arrested and held for the Grand Jury under $1,000 bail.

The charge was selling liquor on Sunday.

It seems that Albert Welch had "the Frenchman" buy him a $1 quart of whiskey from Turner. But when Mrs. Welch "got wind of it", she brought the charges.

Make no mistake. It was the women who had enough of the booze trade and led the march to Prohibition.

The Anti-Saloon League was active in Washington County in 1903, but that did not fore-stall "The 58th annual dance by the Socyal Klub and Hay Rube Boys of Cambridge", at Beach's Hall.

Clearly, there was a battle to be joined. Right-minded husbands took up The Cause. The following week, Fowler's Hall drew a good crowd to hear local big-shots debate the resolution: "That a Prohibition Party is Necessary".

Rev. J.C. Scott of Coila Church and George M. Foster took the affirmative; Robert R. Law and Hiram H. Parrish, good-naturedly for the negative. Naturally, the decision went to the affirmative.

In June of '03, Frank Plunkett, unintimidated and not above rubbing it in, added a "piazza" above the new door he'd sawed into his Raines hotel.

In July, he organized a band of "rowdies", who drunkenly followed the Walter L. Main Circus through the Village streets.

Rev. John G. Smart, taking over from his ailing brother as editor and propietor of the Old WCP, and a "total abstainer", called them "a fiddler and his aggregation of trained animals".

Finally, under the local option provision of the State Constitution then in effect, the East End had enough and voted dry (temporarily).

West End Action

The action then shifted to the West End; that is, those enterprises collected about the intersection of Main and Union Sts.   While White Creek had gone dry, Cambridge accepted the Raines Law.

Under the infamous Raines law, only hotels could be licensed. And a hotel, as it turned out, was any saloon in a building large enough to be chopped into ten or more sleeping rooms.

Cambridge Corners was not above providing its share of boozy hi-jinks.

Local Prohibitionists formed "The Auxiliary Law Enforcement League" to insure that only hotels sold booze in Old Cambridge after May I.

John Agan, "doing a quick change act", converted his illegal saloon into a Raines Hotel.

Outside of Agan's converted saloon one evening after closing time, John Moore found that James Mack had curled up in the bed of Moore's wagon and gone to sleep.

Moore gave him the traditional awakening of tossing him out into the mud of the street. As Mack stood up, Moore whacked him with the butt of his whip, which was a mistake.

Mack "countered in good style by landing a vicious right between the orbs, which had a very soothing effect" upon Moore.

The Post Editor, exhibiting a thin strain of humor, hoped the East Enders were grateful to the West for easing their burden.

John Agan prospered so that he, too, added a piazza to the front of his building.

By August, the crusty Editor Smart termed the West End "a booze haven", primarily at Tom Rogers' establishment. Where exactly this Raines Hotel was located is not known. It may have been the former McMurray's Oyster House, across the street east of the Union House, more likely referred to the Irving House, which was owned for a number of years by the Rogers family.

"Youths from Cohoes and Hoosick Falls who can't hold their beer find his porch and front walk a handy place of 'discharge'," he reported.

"The merchants across Main St. complain of rowdiness and profanity and a smell that laps on the breeze." But they would, he predicted wryly, adjust as the East Enders had.

One of the steady, West End customers was James O'Brien. Jimmy was caught red-handed (literally) in William McMillan's hog pen early one Thursday morning. He was seated in the slop, surrounded be a dozen, carefully selected hens, their heads "rung off" and ready to pop into the sack. Jimmy could run, and did. But being well known, he was "collected" and sent to Salem jail under $500 bond.

Two East-Enders were arrested by Deputy Sheriff Earl Morse and indicted by the county Grand Jury for selling hooch without a license. It was supposedly trucked in by wagon at night from Eagle Bridge.

One was a familiar name: Frank Plunkett; the other was Charles B. Hunt, who operated something called "The Cottage Hotel". They were held for trial under $500 bond.

Booze Buys Town Hall

At his trial, Plunkett was fined $300. Editor Smart noted that Plunkett took out a roll of bills and passed it over without counting, suggesting (l) that a deal had been struck; and (2) that there was money to be made in illegal hooch.

Hunt pled not guilty.

Editor Smart recommended that the Raines Law be thrown out or radically over-hauled. He admitted that its high license approach returned good revenues to the Towns, but it was never intended as a Temperance law.

In fact, Cambridge paid for its Town Hall with revenue returned from the State under this same Raines Law.

That July, a drunken "Polander" ran amock in Buskirk's Bridge. A section hand on the Greenwich and Johnsonville line, he was put off the train. He made a violent invasion of Charles King's house. King and a hired man captured him, bound him with ropes and chains and threw him in the back of a wagon. Then they brought him to the lockup in Cambridge Village.

The lockup is a story unto itself. The first one was down along the railroad track about in back of George Van Hook's house.
The second was in the basement of the Engine House.

The Village wanted the third to be in the defunct Congregational Church, but the remaining members wouldn't consent to it.

The exasperated Editor escaped into nostalgia, recalling when it was a crime to be drunk on the streets of Old Cambridge, with a $5 or $10 fine attached.

"Nowadays," he wrote, "It is impossible to walk from one end to the other without running into one, staggering or fallen."

This was nothing new. It is the way it had been since the Civil War. But slowly the noose was tightening against necks of the unruly and unrepentent booze traders.

In October, 1905, George Wortley, clerk at the Cambridge House, was indicted for violating the excise law. The Cambridge House, being in White Creek, could not sell booze at this time.

Editor Smart reported that the Engine House was being used "for improper purposes". Beer bottles, cards and cigar stubs had been found.

However, the voting majority of both towns (remember, women did not yet vote in general elections) had not yet ceased to support the booze interests.

When the local option question was voted that fall, both White Creek and Cambridge turned down licenses for the old basement saloons and stores, but approved licenses for pharmacies (medicinal) and hotels, by 87 votes in White Creek and only 25 in Cambridge.

There was no vote in Jackson, as that township was bone dry, and stayed that way thru most of the years of conflict.

No Raines Hotels

In April, 1906, Governor Higgins signed a modified excise law to put an end to Raines hotels.

Hence forth, the town supervisor or village president had to inspect and make sure that the licensed establishment was, indeed, in the business of providing lodging and meals, as well as booze, for travelers.

Any citizen thinking that a "Raines hotel" was operating could file a statement with the State Liquor Commissioner, who "must thereupon cause an inspection".

And they did. First the Village Board of Health inspected the Village Raines hotels for proper sewerage, sanitation and fire escapes. Then Village President William Eldridge looked them over.   Those hotels that passed inspection opened for business; those that did not scrambled to comply with the new requirements.

Editor Smart right away challenged the application of Charles B. Hunt. He sought a license for his "cottage" on East Main. But is it a hotel? asked the Editor. Since Hunt had been in jail under the indictment, it had been a fish market, he noted.

The license was taken off the wall of William Sheridan's "hotel" on W. Main. This business was where the Ed Levin jewelry manufactory was in 2010. Sheridan lacked one of the required 10 bedrooms, which he quickly tacked on.

That May, 1906, Drs. McMillan and Niver declined to respond to calls at late hours to help drunks. They had too many bad experiences.

In June was made one of several changes over the years in the grade of West Main. "The cutting down of the Union House knoll" allowed for the removal of the boardwalks from both sides of the street and the laying down of a proper walk, with --- one would suspect --- a negative impact on the basement saloons along the street.

A new fountain went in at Main and Union, between the sidewalk and the street. It would be accessible on all sides. Pedestrians would there-after be able to pass along the front of the hotel "without horses slobbering all over them".

Later, as the Raines Hotels began to attract all the trade from the East End, some "wag" dubbed Cambridge Corners "San Juan Hill", noting that there had been numerous "eruptions" among the drunks.

But there was a large and growing opposition to the booze halls.

The Crusades

Following Memorial Day, in 1905, Prohibitionists brought a week-long crusade to Hubbard's Hall. Tennyson Smith of NYCity was the featured speaker each night. His sermons were of the horror of saloons;, rather full of pathos and humor, Editor Smart thought. Smith prided himself on being an extemporaneous speaker, which the editor took to mean "it all came out the same".

Mock trials being all the rage, the Prohibitionists tried "alcohol" the last night.

That May, Charles Anson Ingraham, an Old Cambridge boy, published a history of the Temperance movement.

The first of October, 400 attended another Prohibition rally at Hubbard's Hall. With the hotels and Inns depending upon liquor for much of their trade, Hubbard's Hall was about the only "neutral territory" available to the Prohibitionists.

Women at the Fore

The opposition to booze halls and the liquor interests was led, primarily, by the women. Many were of a militant turn of mind already, as they were still battling for voting rights. And as no respectable woman could enter a saloon, there was no reason for them to look with tolerance upon the foiblous nature of men.

As the battle raged, a peculiar thing happened. Even the men got sick of it. Toleration toward alcohol completely evaporated.

The year 1899 was a tough time for local hotels. Frank McMurray, Irving House lessee from Greenwich, "decamped" right after the fair closed, "Leaving behind a number of creditors to regret their brief acquaintance with him".

McMurray had leased "on promises" that August 23, just in time for the fair, and had bought the contents of the bar from the hotel owner, D.C. Stroud. He promised installments would be paid fair week.

The bar trade was good. The stock was reduced, so Stroud replenished it.

Local businessmen supplied McMurray "on tick". Three Albany brewers lent him $150 each to get started.

The first (and only) check McMurray wrote Mr. Stroud was for $100 on a Vermont bank "of questionable worth".

As Stroud pressed him during fair week, at one point McMurray showed Stroud a thick roll and dared him to try to get it.

That same night, McMurray packed and left, destination unknown.

Of course, the Vermont check was no good and Stroud was out more than $1,000.

Herb Malloy of Bennington was the next lessee. The neighbors had enough and tried to oppose the issuing of his liquor license, to no avail.

Mary Hubbard Active

Mary Hubbard was still active in the women's movement. In February, 1900, she went to Washington for the national conventions of both the DAR and the WCTU.

The culminating year for Old Cambridge was the year 1909.   That October, 1909 a series of Sabbath services were devoted to defeating liquor licensing at the polls.

The third week of the month, women of the community rallied in Hubbard's Hall for the Temperance cause. The grand old Hall was packed. Strident, Christian hymns rang to the plaster ceilings, sending a thrill up every stiffened spine.

Ministers exhorted. Elocutionists declaimed. Fervent prayers winged to the Almighty, who (at last) smiled upon their enterprise.

Out on Main St. before the Hall, they organized into a procession. Then they marched and counter-marched through the Village. Up Main St. to Dorr's Corners they went, bravely past the hell-holes of Plunkett and Hunt, and beyond the dark barroom of the ancient Irving House.

Turning, they marched in full defiance the length of Main St. back to Academy, running the gauntlet of Raines Hotels, whose drunken patrons jeered and staggered from the sidewalks.

The Cambridge Band led. R. L. Beveridge was parade marshal. School kids and civic organizations joined in the holy crusade.   There were many walkers. There were many carriages. There was even one automobile, relegated to the rear, lest it frighten the horses.

There were many banners, bearing the various slogans of "The Sacred Cause":

"Rally, Rally All You Free men!"
"God is Leading to the Battle!"
"Protect Our Home!"
"There is No Time to Lose!"
"Don't Vote Your Boys Away!'
"Save the Children, Save the State!"
"Rally All, Or Wrong Will Rule in the State!"
"Save the Boys!"
"In God We Trust!"

The grand old Hall was filled. The militant, Christian hymns rang to the plaster ceilings and sent a thrill up every spine.

Ministers exhorted. Moving verses were declaimed. Fervent prayers went up to the Almighty, who surely must have smiled benevolently upon their theme.

The White Creek Village Temperance Assoc. met at that same time at the Methodist Church. They set out to organize a Law and Order League.

Their efforts, and those of hundreds of thousands of concerned citizens across the Nation, paid off at the polls.

As the polls closed and word of the results swept like rumor across the Towns, one by one, the church bells of every hamlet and village began to ring.

In both Cambridge and White Creek the forces for no booze licenses had triumphed.

Old Cambridge went dry, as dry as the law could make it and the conscientious efforts of its citizenry keep it.

Of the four categories of licenses that citizens were asked to consider, all were defeated. Jackson was already dry; so, for the next year there would be no legal, beverage alcohol, not even medicinal, available in Old Cambridge.

Hotel licensing was defeated in White Creek by 15 votes, in Cambridge by 64.

Cambridge voted 156-220 against licensing hotels to sell booze; 113-235 against licensing saloons; 145-194 against allowing the sale of alcohol from drug stores for medicinal purposes and 107-216 against licensing stores.

White Creek went 149-229 against hotels, 128-285 against saloons, 268-283 against drug store sales and 98-276 against grocery store sales.

Editor John G. Smart, who himself practiced total abstinence, was as exultant as the rest. Never in the history of the Village has there been anything like it, he wrote.

"The Temperance cyclone, which for a year or two past, has been sweeping... the West and the South clear of the saloon,
...has reached us."

The new law would go into effect in a year, October, 1910.

Smart was not so exhiliarated that he lost touch with the realities. Now, he wrote, we must organize to enforce the law!

If Mary Nye Hubbard could have lived but two months longer, she could have tasted the sweet fruits born of a life-time devoted to the causes of Suffrage and Temperance.

The following week, victories "dries" gathered at the Engine House to form a Law and Order League, the second such vigilante organization in the history of the community. Its object was to secure the enforcement of the excise law and the punishment of all crime.

C.E. Smith was president, R. L. Beveridge veep.

There was an executive committee to represent the League "in legal proceedings", meaning that they intended to press charges themselves, where the police and sheriff would not.

As history records, the "victory" was won, but the "battle" was lost.